PSALMS
Conversations with God

Let the word of Christ dwell in you richly as you teach and admonish one another with all wisdom, and as you sing psalms, hymns and spiritual songs with gratitude in your hearts to God (Colossians 3:16).

Compiled by Debb Andrus

Donald Hoeferkamp, Project Editor

Thomas J. Doyle, Series Editor

CPH
SAINT LOUIS

Unless otherwise indicated, Scripture quotations are from the HOLY BIBLE, NEW INTERNA-
TIONAL VERSION®. Copyright © 1973, 1978, 1984 by the International Bible Society. Used
by permission of Zondervan Publishing House. All rights reserved.

The "NIV" and "New International Version" trademarks are registered in the United States
Patent and Trademark Office by the International Bible Society. Use of either trademark
requires the permission of the International Bible Society.

Bible references marked TLB are from THE LIVING BIBLE, © 1971 by Tyndale House Pub-
lishers, Wheaton, IL. Used by permission.

Contents

Lesson 1

God Speaks to Assure Me of His Existence (Psalm 19)

Aims

To know God through the world He created, through His Word, and through experiences with Him.

To gain assurance that God will sustain us through our life.

Purpose

The purpose of this study is to help us hear God's message every time we read His Word. It is possible to read without hearing. We want to learn to let God speak very personally to us as we read the psalms.

What Is a Psalm?

A psalm is a song or poem distinguished by its devotional character and deep piety. It is the faith of the Old Testament set to music, a poem springing from an encounter with God. It is worship literature.

It is Hebrew poetry, and Hebrew poetry is different from English poetry. To us poetry must have meter, and it usually rhymes. Hebrew poetry is not concerned with meter and rhyme but instead uses many *parallelisms*, in which the same thought is expressed in various ways. It also uses many word *pictures*, *contrasts*, and *repetitions*.

Studying the Psalm

A. David Sees God's Hand in Creation (Psalm 19:1–6)

What were some of the things in nature that declared the glory of God, the Creator? Remember that in the days when the psalms were written the Hebrews did not have the faintest idea of what we today call "natural laws." They thought that everything in nature was due to the direct activity of God—whether it was a storm or a drought, springtime or harvest. Have there been losses, as well as gains, in the scientific understanding of the universe today? If so, what are they?

1. What two voices tell us of God (**v. 1**)?
What two verbs does the writer use in **verse 1?**
Here we have a perfect example of a parallelism. Both sentences mean the same thing and yet are expressed in different words. We will see parallelisms in all the psalms.

2. In **verses 2–4a** David shows ways in which nature's message to us is so wonderful: It is like a continued story, never ending.
   a. When is it heard (**v. 2**)? _____ and
_____
   b. The message does not come to us by (**v. 3**) _____
_____ or _____, and yet we get the message that God is the great Creator.

   c. Nature's voice is not limited to continents. Where can it be heard (**v. 4**)?
(Note that in **Romans 10:18** Paul quotes this verse. Also note the picture of a tent in **Isaiah 40:22** and **Psalm 104:2.**)

3. As a special wonder of creation, David refers to the sun. Hebrew poetry is full of word pictures. What pictures does David use to describe the sun (**v. 5**)?

B. David Sees God in the Word (Psalm 19:7–11)

The Word, as David knew it, was not the Bible as we know it today. The Law, or the Torah (the five books of Moses), was held in high regard and was reverenced with great awe. What was God like to the people of the Old Testament?

1. From **verses 7–11,** list six words that mean "the Word of God" and the description of each:

Words	Descriptions
_____	_____
_____	_____
_____	_____
_____	_____
_____	_____
_____	_____

(The phrase "fear of the Lord" is not well known to us as a phrase designating the Scriptures. See **Proverbs 15:33.**)

2. List four things the Word of God accomplishes in us:

3. How is the preciousness of God's Word described in **verse 10?**

4. Why is God's Word so valuable **(v. 11)?**

C. David Sees God in a Personal Experience of Forgiveness (Psalm 19:12–14)

The psalm closes with a series of petitions of great importance to a healthy faith life.

1. For what is David praying in **verses 12–13?**

2. State in your own words what David says in **verse 14.**

3. What does David call God?

God Speaks to Me

1. Having studied **Psalm 19,** what would you answer a person who says, "I don't need to read the Bible or go to church. I can go fishing Sunday mornings and worship God in nature"?

2. What words come to mind about God the Creator when you see the beauties of nature?

3. Suggest ways in which God has revealed Himself to you in (1) nature, (2) the Word, (3) a relationship with another Christian.

4. How can this psalm give you confidence as you enter each new day of your life?

More Understanding

(You may greatly enrich your understanding by doing some of the following supplemental suggestions.)

The message of this psalm (and indeed all of God's Word) is more clear if the meaning of the words is known. Don't be afraid to use your dictionary! Also, because one part of the Bible throws light on other parts, use a Bible and concordance for cross-references. Use other translations of the Bible too.

You may wish to read more about psalms in a Bible dictionary or commentaries.

1. Note how the heavens speak of God's glory day and night, like a continued story. Look at **Psalm 8:3–4.** What question did the sights of the night suggest to the psalmist? Look at **Matthew 6:28–29** and note what daytime beauty Jesus used to teach a lesson.

2. What does the psalmist mean by these phrases **(Psalm 19:7–8):**

"reviving the soul"? Look in your dictionary. See **Isaiah 57:15** for additional understanding.

"making wise the simple"? See **Psalm 119:130; 1 Corinthians 1:25–26; Colossians 1:9; James 1:5.**

"giving joy to the heart"? See **Psalm 51:12; 32:11.**

"giving light to the eye"? See **Ephesians 1:18; John 1:9.**

3. Compare the prayer in **Psalm 19:14** with the prayer in **Psalm 104:34.**

Lesson 2

God Speaks
When I Am Frightened
(Psalm 46)

Aims

To look realistically at the present world situation.
To see our security as children of God in this world.

Purpose

Civilians are caught in the crossfire of warring factions . . . Nuclear weapons are in the control of small countries that are struggling for power . . . Two-thirds of the world's population will go to bed hungry tonight . . . Fire destroys a home and burns children . . . Race riots tear apart cities . . . Governments are overthrown . . . and so it goes. No matter which day you pick up a newspaper, the headlines scream frightening news and remind us that we live in a world beset with situations that leave us frightened and sick at heart.

Psalm 46 has been called the psalm of "holy confidence" for God's people. One author says, "As **1 Corinthians 13** may be called the sublime hymn of love, this psalm may be called the sublime hymn of faith." No matter what threatening circumstances there have been—personal, national, or international—people have found new courage when they have read this psalm. Even during the turbulent days of the Reformation, when Melanchthon would express fear lest the Reformation be stilled before it got under way, Luther would say, "Come, Philip, let us sing the 46th Psalm." This was his source of confidence. The psalm was also his inspiration for the great hymn of the Reformation, "A Mighty Fortress Is Our

God." Perhaps this study will enable us also to say that this is our psalm of "holy confidence."

Note the structure of this psalm: **verses 1–3, verses 4–7, verses 8–11.** These are three distinct and purposeful divisions. You will note that **verses 7** and **11** are identical and are refrains to the second and third parts. Although the exact meaning of the word *Selah* is not known, it is apparently a direction to the singers for a pause or a break of some sort. It may even have been some particular instruction. Note the repetition of this word at the close of each section.

Studying the Psalm

A. Confidence in the Midst of Commotion (vv. 1–3)

An important lesson to learn about the conquest of fear is that our first step is to face the threatening person or circumstance realistically. Don't try to forget, deny, or run away from fear. The psalmist faced very honestly the fact of trouble in the world and humankind's natural reaction.

1. What was the trouble and commotion pictured by the psalmist? If you were writing this psalm today, what images would you use in order to convey an impression of chaos? What specific situations and incidents in the world would you have in mind?

2. What was the psalmist's confidence in the midst of this commotion? Not all the trouble and commotion in the world are as remote as mountain slides, earthquakes, floods, wars, etc. Much of it is very personal. What are the circumstances of trouble and commotion in your personal "world"? How can you have confidence when it seems that your world is crumbling and falling in upon you? In what ways have you experienced God as your refuge and strength in times like this?

B. God's Glad City (vv. 4–7)

Here is a contrast to the first picture of commotion. This is a picture of God's grace and peace flowing in the midst of His people, making them glad.

1. In what sense is the picture of a river flowing into the city a picture of the calm refreshing of God's grace?

2. In contrast to the commotion described in **verses 1–3,** what does the presence of God promise **(v. 5)?**

3. In contrast to the unstable power of the nations and kingdoms, how does the psalmist describe God's power **(v. 6)?**

4. Note the names of God in **verse 7.** What do they indicate about the characteristics of God? (Note also the verbs in this verse.)

Read **verses 4–7** again. Do you think that the second section of this psalm can have any real meaning for a person who has just been diagnosed as having a terminal disease? for a family whose house has been destroyed by a tornado? How does the "river" of God's grace and peace bring stability and confidence to a Christian in any situation?

C. Invitation to See God at Work (vv. 8–11)

We are invited to see God at work in the world. He is always active. This psalm is full of word pictures to describe His activity.

1. How do **verses 8** and **9** reveal God's involvement in the world?

2. In the midst of war, confusion, and trouble God is also speaking. What does He say **(v. 10)?**

Why do we not hear Him?

3. What confidence can we draw from **verses 10–11?**

Read **verses 8–11** again. How does stopping to look and meditate upon God's activity and listening to Him speak become a source of strength? Is God exalted in the world today? Why or why not?

God Speaks Today

1. Is it easier or more difficult to believe in God's presence with His people today than it was in the days of the psalmist? What makes you think so?

2. For what do you pray in times of distress? Be specific and think of one particular difficult situation in your life. Were you aware of God? Was He of any help in the situation?

3. What important thought did this psalm leave with you? (Note the reaffirmation of faith in **verse 11**.)

More Understanding

You may enrich your understanding by doing the following:

1. Using pencil and paper, write down the parallelisms in each verse, the phrases or sentences following one another. Try to determine if they are in contrast to one another, saying the same thing in different words, or enriching one another. You may wish to read in a commentary or dictionary about the types of parallelisms in the psalms. You may also wish to read more widely on the construction of Hebrew poetry.

2. Make a list of all the phrases, descriptions, and names of God in this psalm. How does meditating on these give us confidence in the midst of our troubled world?

3. See what you can find to enrich your understanding of the phrase "the city of God" and the concepts and meanings of the second section of this psalm (vv. 4–7). For a real challenge look at Augustine's book *The City of God*, which may be found in some libraries.

4. Study the hymn "A Mighty Fortress Is Our God" to understand Martin Luther's confidence and trust in God as reflected in this hymn. What characteristics of God does he stress? If you have a book on the history and meaning of hymns, this one is no doubt included.

5. How would you summarize the message of this psalm in one sentence?

Lesson 3

God Speaks about the Suffering Messiah (Psalm 22)

Aims

To see the struggle and victory of the psalmist.
To see how Christ fulfilled this psalm on the cross.
To look to Christ in hours of darkness.

Purpose

To "keep Lent" is an expression often used during the 40 days preceding Easter. What we usually mean is that we observe the season in some special way. The most meaningful way is to permit the Scriptures to take us to Calvary to spend time beneath the cross.

Have you ever glanced at **Psalm 22** and wondered why you found the same words Christ spoke from the cross and what connection there might be between the two? If you are like a multitude of readers, you merely thought "How strange!" and let it go at that. In this study we want to look at Christ's use of these words.

Messianic Psalms

Psalm 22 is one of a number of psalms that are messianic in character; that is, psalms that point to the Messiah. It is important that you remember two facts about messianic psalms: (1) The psalmists were inspired to write words true of themselves in their particular situation, and (2) only in Christ are these words perfectly fulfilled.

Jesus Himself said, "Everything must be fulfilled that is written *about*

Me in the Law of Moses, the prophets and the *psalms*" (**Luke 24:44,** emphasis added).

Studying the Psalm

I. The Story of the Psalm

In **Psalm 22** David speaks of his own afflictions without knowing that the Holy Spirit led him to express his feelings in words that Christ would later speak from the cross.

Read the whole psalm. Note that it is divided clearly into two parts: in **verses 1–21,** when David's cry of anguish goes unanswered, his mood goes down, down, down; in **verses 22–31,** David's mood goes up, up, up when God seems to answer him. Then David bursts forth in a song of praise. What accounts for this change of tone?

A. David's Cry of Anguish (vv. 1–21)

Read **verses 1–21** with David in mind.

1. What are some of the phrases David uses to describe his anguish?

2. What two questions does he ask of God **(v. 1)?**

3. What is the result of his crying to God **(v. 2)?**

4. The psalmist clings to the memory of past help. Who received this help **(vv. 4–5)?**

5. What repeated word describes their relationship to God (vv. 4–5)?

6. How did God respond to their cry (vv. 4–5)?

7. How did the psalmist contrast himself with his fathers (v. 6)? What did he call himself?

8. What was David's relationship to God from his very birth (vv. 9–10)?

9. How does David describe his condition (vv. 14–15)? What do these expressions mean to you?

10. What are his enemies doing to him now (vv. 16–18)?

11. Sometimes when you are faced with serious problems in life and feel forsaken by God, what lifts you up again? What help might this psalm give you? When you are frustrated or discouraged or feeling guilty, what do you have in your memory to help you rise out of the deep?

B. David's Song of Praise (vv. 22–31)

1. Note the change of mood. Begin with the psalmist's own declaration of thanks and praise and trace the ever-widening circle of people and nations he invites to join in his doxology following his deliverance:

Verse 22: I will . . .

Verse 23: You . . . praise Him

Verse 25: _____

Verse 27: _____

Verse 28: _____

Verse 29: _____

Verse 30: _____

Verse 31: _____

2. Note that even before David is delivered out of his distress, he turns in confidence to God in a doxology of praise and thanksgiving **(vv. 22–31)**. In taking hold again of his faith, which had seemed to slip away from him, he was brought to assurance and reaffirmation of faith. This resulted in joy and confidence. People in distress or grief often ask, "Why?" What is the difference between rebellion against God when disaster strikes and David's questioning in his struggle to understand? What have you struggled to understand in your relationship with God? What was the result?

II. Christ and This Psalm

Reread the psalm with Christ in mind, especially **verses 14–18.**

A. What foresights of Christ's suffering and death do you see? What was accomplished by Christ as He was forsaken by His Father?

B. What foresights of Christ's ministry and the spread of His Gospel do you see in **verses 22–31?**

III. Parallel Experiences of David and Jesus

Read **2 Samuel 15:23, 30** and **John 18:1**. What similarity of experience do you see? Read **Matthew 27:35–46** and **John 19:23–37** and find in **Psalm 22** all the parallel experiences of David and of Christ upon the cross.

IV. David's Enemies Compared to Wild Animals (vv. 12, 13, 16, 20, 21)

The psalmist describes animals to complete the picture of his suffering. In your group, discuss what you know about the animals listed. What image is David trying to show by each?

Verse 12: _____

Verses 13, 21a: _____

Verses 16, 20: _____

Verse 21b: _____

V. David's Physical and Emotional Suffering (vv. 14–15)

Have you ever had to endure severe physical or emotional suffering? What was your physical reaction to such suffering? Read how David describes himself in response to the suffering he was enduring.

VI. How Help Came (v. 21)

What lifted David out of his depression? (Note that in **verse 21** "save me" can also be translated as "You have heard me." See also **Psalm 3:4**.)

VII. The Poor Will Eat (v. 26)

David uses the rest of the psalm to describe how he will praise and thank God. What are some things you do to praise and thank God? How does David's statement that the poor will eat show praise and thanksgiving to God?

VIII. "He Has Done It" (v. 31)

How did Jesus fulfill the last four words of the psalm? (See **John 19:30.**) What important thought did this psalm leave with you?

More Understanding

1. Read **1** and **2 Samuel** for information about the life of David.

2. David appeals to God as one who has been a Father to him since his birth. Read **Psalm 139:13–16** and note that David praises God that He had a plan for him even before he was born.

3. Some other messianic psalms you may want to study are **Psalms 2, 8, 16, 45, 72, 110.**

4. How would you summarize the message of **Psalm 22** in your own words?

Lesson 4

God Speaks
about Forgiveness
(Psalm 32)

Aims

To learn what to do with sin and guilt.

To see the consequences of neglected guilt.

To rejoice in God's abundant forgiveness through Christ.

Purpose

Psalm 32 is one of the best-known of the seven penitential psalms (6, 32, 38, 51, 102, 130, 143), in which sin is confessed and forgiveness experienced. Forgiveness brings great joy to the forgiven sinner. Penitent people are willing to admit they have done wrong, are sorry for their wrongs, and are willing to make amends. Then God in His love deals with the sins and brings release and joy to the hearts of the penitent.

Release from guilt is a very important subject because living in guilt has dangerous consequences, including estrangement from God and undue tension.

Should it be necessary to have a Bible study on the subject of release from guilt when every Sunday we say together in the creed, "I believe in . . . the forgiveness of sins," and pray, "O most merciful God . . . have mercy on us and . . . grant us forgiveness of all our sins" or another such confession? Strangely enough, it is necessary! Too many of us who recite these words every Sunday do not actually know how to receive that forgiveness and to live in newness of life.

Someone has said, "The Gospel is not *good advice* but *good news*." We need more than instructions on how to live the good life because we can never be "good enough." What we need is the good news that there is one who can forgive sin, take evil out of our hearts, and put a new and right spirit within us.

Studying the Psalm

A. Forgiveness Brings Blessedness (Psalm 32:1–2)

Note how **verses 1** and **2** mean the same thing but use different words. This is a parallelism. The repetition of thought is for emphasis.

1. The psalmist begins with an outburst of joy. Why was he so happy? Have you had a similar experience that you can share with the group?

2. Compare the first two verses to the last verse of the psalm. Substituting for the word *Blessed* the phrase "Oh, how happy," how would you tell a child what the psalmist is trying to say?

3. What words does the psalmist use for sin? Why does he use them?

4. How does God deal with sin?

B. The Consequences of Unconfessed Sin (vv. 3–4)

Having begun with an outburst of gratitude for forgiveness, the psalmist looks back, as it were, at his condition before he confessed. (Read **2 Samuel 11–12** to recall David's great sin.)

1. "Dangerous Silence" is a title we could use for these two verses. List the kinds of physical and emotional pain caused by David's unconfessed sin.

2. Is it possible that some mental and emotional illness might be directly attributable to guilt and unconfessed sin? What psychological problems can be brought on by guilt in one's life?

C. Confession Brings Forgiveness (v. 5)
1. "Whenever man is ready to uncover his sin, God is ready to cover it." With what words did David show his readiness to uncover sin?

Note that upon confession God immediately forgave.

2. Each Sunday in our liturgy we are helped to confess our sin. Note that in some confession liturgies the pastor and congregation share in the words from the last half of **verse 5.** What do these words mean to you?

3. One writer says that the process of forgiveness includes the following: contrition, confession, absolution, and amendment. What do you think this means, and how does it compare with your experience?

4. How would you pray for a person living in false security who is unconcerned about his or her sin problem? How would you help a person who says, "I don't feel like a sinner; I'm living a decent life"? How would you help a person who prays for forgiveness and never "feels" forgiven?

5. What would happen in families or between friends if members were to learn the important words "I'm sorry"?

D. Exhortation (vv. 6–9)

1. David now calls to all of us, "Do it!" Saint John says the same thing to us. Every Christian should know these verses. Write out and memorize **1 John 1:8–9:**

2. According to **verse 7,** what does God do?

3. **Verses 8–9** may be the psalmist speaking, passing on the instructions of the Lord, or it could be God Himself speaking. What things are promised?

4. In his instructions not to be stubborn, what picture does the psalmist use?

E. Rejoice (vv. 10–11)

Contrast the mental state of the wicked and of the righteous. What have you learned about forgiveness of sins in this study?

More Understanding

You may greatly enrich your understanding by doing some of the following supplemental suggestions.

1. Study these penitential psalms: **6; 38; 51; 102; 130;** and **143,** noting the similarities and differences between these and **Psalm 32.**

2. In a dictionary look up other words used for "sin" such as *iniquity, guilt, deceit, debt, transgression,* etc. Look up the words for "forgiveness": *imputation, cover, deliverance.*

3. Read about David in **1** and **2 Samuel,** especially his experience of sin and guilt in **2 Samuel 11–12.** In **Psalm 32** David describes the emotional and physical results of guilt that he experienced. See also **Psalm 62:2–7** and **Psalm 51:8.** Compare his confession in **Psalm 32:5** with that in **Psalm 51:3.**

4. Study **Romans 4** and note the use of **Psalm 32:1–2.** What is the point of its inclusion there?

Lesson 5

God Speaks
When I Am Moody
(Psalms 42 and 43)

Aims

To see the cause for moods and affirm its cure.

Purpose

In the creation story God said, "Let us make man in our image" (**Genesis 1:26**). We are God-planned, God-made. Just like God Himself, we have intellect and a will with which to make choices; we have emotions. Most of all we need to know God's nearness and His love. We long for fellowship with Him.

A statement worth remembering, probably spoken by Augustine, an early church father, is this: "God has reserved in every human heart a vacancy that He alone can fill." How empty are those who try to fill this vacancy with substitutes. Some try to still the longing with education, others with possessions, others with success or honor. But they are never completely satisfied. They always reach out for something that eludes them. With Christ in the heart, there is peace and contentment even though the possessions are few. The vacancy is filled. The longing is stilled.

Psalms 42 and **43** are one composition. The thought of **Psalm 42** is continued in **Psalm 43.** The two main topics to keep in mind are (1) people's longing for God, and (2) people's moods in the midst of trouble and their hope in God. The psalmist shows us how he feels in three difficult life situations:

1. When he is excluded from the temple service where he wanted to be, and also when he is mocked for his longing for God (**42:1–5**).

2. When he finds that he is miles away from where he longed to be, and

he feels forgotten by God—and for this, too, his enemies mock him (**42:6–11**).

3. When he must live and deal with difficult people (**43**).

Look at each of these situations and see what you can learn for your own life situation.

Studying the Psalms

A. The Psalmist Longs for God (42:1–5)

1. Note the psalmist's state of mind. List the words that describe his frustration (**vv. 1–3**).

2. What question does he ask (**v. 2**)?

3. What questions do people ask of him (**v. 3**)?

4. What memories plague the psalmist (**v. 4**)?

5. What is the meaning of **verses 1–5?** Whether the psalmist's longing was for the temple worship itself or more probably for the presence of God is not too significant. We know there is a deep longing for some kind of communion with God. What situation in life might bring a feeling of separation from God in our experience? Could illness or physical isolation make one feel far from God? What longings do you sometimes feel? Do you really long for God Himself or only for His gifts? How can memories of the

past encourage us at such times? Does it really bother you to be deprived of the privilege of worship with fellow Christians?

6. Note the refrain in **verse 5** and the tone of hope it introduces.

B. The Psalmist Feels Forgotten by God (42:6–11)

1. The psalmist is far from the temple and is unable to attend temple worship. In what mood is the psalmist now **(vv. 6–9)?**

2. How does he describe the pile-up of trouble **(v. 7)?**

3. To what hope does he turn **(v. 8)?**

4. Note the repeated refrain in **verse 11.**

5. The psalmist felt so far removed from God that he felt he was actually forgotten. This could happen to us as well. Have you ever felt forgotten by God in some dire situation? What did you do?

C. The Psalmist Prays for Restored Joy (43)
1. In what mood is he now **(v. 2)**?

2. Who troubles him now **(v. 1)?**

3. To what two questions does he seek an answer **(v. 2)?**

4. Not being able to change his situation or the difficult people with whom he is associated, for what does he ask **(v. 3)?**

5. Where will light and truth bring him **(v. 4)?**

6. What will this do to his moods **(v. 4)?**

7. Still today we face many times when people are unsympathetic to our longing for God and the things of the kingdom. We often live and deal with difficult people, both inside and outside the church. What kind of persecution have you experienced from people with whom you live or work who do not understand your situation? How did you react?

8. Three times the psalmist takes himself to task, trying to shake off his mood of dejection and frustration. In the repeated refrains (42:5, 11 and 43:5), what does he ask himself and what solution does he find for his troubles?

9. The great lesson of this psalm may be to know how to handle our moods and feelings of despondency and despair. What can we learn from the psalmist that can help us? How does the repeated refrain help?

10. How does the writer express his certainty of this hope?

11. How would you summarize the message of this psalm in one sentence?

More Understanding

1. Read a commentary on these psalms, if possible.

2. Note the many times the psalmist refers to meeting with God in the temple service: "When can I go and meet with God," "leading the procession to the house of God," "I will yet praise Him," "bring me to Your holy mountain," "I go to the altar of God," "to God." To understand the psalmist's deep longing for the temple service, we need to know what the

temple and the service were like. Read **2 Chronicles 5:12–14; 1 Chronicles 23:2–6; Exodus 28:2–4, 40–41;** and **Psalm 22:25.** Try to imagine what feelings came to the worshipers as they entered the temple, heard thrilling music, and saw vast crowds of worshipers.

3. What is the meaning of the statement "My tears have been my food"? (See **Psalm 6:6; 56:8; 80:5.**)

4. With pencil and paper go through **Psalm 42** and **Psalm 43** again, jotting down on one side of your paper all the phrases that describe the despondency and despair of the psalmist and on the other side all the words and phrases that describe his hope.

Lesson 6

God Speaks about the Great Creator (Psalm 104)

Aims

To become more aware of beauty around us.

To think of God when we see beauty.

To demonstrate joy as our thoughts linger on the beauty of God's creation and His love for us in Christ.

Purpose

We today are a traveling people. In the summer we flock to lakes and mountains in our own land or in foreign countries. Happily, most of us go well-armed with cameras and camcorders. We often come back with hundreds of pictures of places and objects of beauty. Home again, we invite neighbors and friends to come and see what we have seen of beauty in the world. Even those of us who do not get to faraway places, upon seeing a lovely rose in the garden or a bird on a branch, run for the camera to capture a moment of wondrous sight. How true are the words of John Keats, "A thing of beauty is a joy forever."

What does all this beauty say to us? Sometimes we simply say, "That was a beautiful view!" But the psalmist reacted to beauty by saying, "How many are Your works, O Lord! In wisdom You made them all" **(Psalm 104:24).** The poet Babcock, in the familiar hymn "This Is My Father's World," says, "He speaks to me everywhere."

Read **Psalm 104,** noting these three divisions:

God, the Creator of the earth **(vv. 1–13)**

The fruitfulness of the earth **(vv. 14–23)**

God, the sustainer of life **(vv. 24–35)**

This is one of the great psalms about nature. Some others are **8;19:1–6; and 29.** As we study the wonders of God's creation, we will compare this psalm with the creation account in the first chapter of the Bible. With the eyes of the psalmist let us look at the world in which we live as God's great handiwork, and let us praise His greatness, honor, and majesty.

Studying the Psalm

A. The Heavens (vv. 1–4)

As you read these verses, look for some of the activities that reveal the greatness of God in creation. (Note the verbs.) Share experiences from your observation of nature that have led you to a new awareness of the greatness of God.

1. What is the first phenomenon in nature that the psalmist mentions **(v. 2)?** See **Genesis 1:3.** What were God's first words of creation?

2. What other acts of God does the psalmist list **(vv. 2–4)?** (See **Genesis 1:6–7** and **Amos 9:6.**)

B. The Earth (vv. 5–9)

The psalmist describes God's creation of the earth. What power did God use? (See also **Genesis 1:9; 7:17–20;** and **9:11–15.**)

C. The Water (vv. 10–13)

1. What are some uses for water, as listed in these verses?

2. In **verse 10** note that the psalmist speaks about springs. Why are they so important?

(See the importance of water as recorded in **Genesis 2:5–6.**)

In the land of Palestine one of the greatest gifts of God is water. Consequently, the Palestinian people came to appreciate water in a way that we may not. Think of all the ways you have used water during the past week. How would life have been different if the water had been turned off in your area? Can you think of areas in the world where there is a serious water shortage today? What is happening as a result? How about the water pollution problem or our wastefulness of this natural resource? What is our obligation?

D. Vegetation (vv. 14–18)

Notice all the things that God provides for humans and animals for a full life. What is our role and obligation in this fruitful world? How can we account for poverty in a world where God has provided so abundantly?

(Compare to **Genesis 1:11–12, 29–30.**)

E. Moon and Sun (vv. 19–23)

1. Why is the moon important to people?

2. Why is darkness a part of God's good provision?

3. How is daylight to be used by people?

F. The Sea (vv. 24–26)
1. What is found in the sea?

2. What is man-made that goes upon the sea?

3. In a dictionary look up the meaning of the word *leviathan.*

G. Life (vv. 27–30)
1. Who are "these all" **(vv. 27–28)** who have been mentioned in **verses 14–26?**

2. In what way do they look to the Creator? How has God planned for the continuance of life in His creation? How can you say that God is good when He has planned creation in such a way that the balance of nature necessitates that one animal lives by killing another?

3. What happens when God withdraws provision **(v. 29)?**

4. How does God renew the earth **(v. 30)?**

H. Praise to the Creator (vv. 31–35)
1. What two wishes does the psalmist express in **verse 31?** (See **Genesis 1:31.**)

2. The psalmist remembers that God can destroy the world He made. What two examples of God's power does he point out in **verse 32?**

3. The wonders of nature fill the psalmist with delight. How will he express this **(vv. 33–34)?**

4. In the study of this psalm, what have you learned about God, and in what way has it stimulated an upsurge of praise? Families can learn together to appreciate God's creation. Mention ways this can be done. Nature poetry is one means of opening our eyes to the wonders in the world. How can such poems be used at home, at camp, at church?

5. What important thought did this psalm leave with you?

More Understanding

1. For additional descriptions of God's wonders of creation, read **Job 38–41.** God uses a display of His creative ability to convince Job that He can do all things and that no purpose of His can be thwarted.

2. Study **Psalm 29** imagining yourself in a fierce thunderstorm. What would you see? Read it again, imagining the rain coming at the end of drought, bringing peace and blessing. Let the psalm assure you that God still reveals Himself in the majesty of the storm and that we are dependent upon Him for every good and perfect gift.

3. Study **Psalm 8,** which is **Genesis 1** set to music. In this psalm note especially how God is praised as the Creator of humankind. Creating man and woman was God's crowning act of creation. Compare **Job 7:17** and **Psalm 144:3.**

4. In this world of beauty the psalmist wishes there were no disharmony. He wants God to remove those who bring evil into this beautiful world. Who are they **(v. 35)?**

Lesson 7

God Speaks
about National Distress
(Psalms 124 and 67)

Aims

To see where help for a nation is to be found.
To be encouraged to pray more faithfully for our country.

Purpose

We Christians are aware that we are citizens of two kingdoms: our own country and the kingdom of God. This is dramatized by the two flags in our churches. In the U.S.A., citizens express their loyalty to their country in these words:

I pledge allegiance to the flag of the United States of America and to the Republic for which it stands, one Nation under God, indivisible, with liberty and justice for all.

We can express our loyalty to the kingdom of God in these words:

I pledge allegiance to the Christian flag and to the Savior for whose kingdom it stands, one Savior, crucified, risen and coming again, with life and liberty for all who believe.

"May God be gracious to us" should be on the lips of all citizens daily as they face enemies from without (hostile nations, nuclear warheads) and enemies from within (corruption, violence, alcoholism, delinquency, racial tensions, broken homes). "May God be gracious to us" should also be the prayer of every citizen during every election. As responsible citizens, let us humbly ask God to help us elect the people of His choice.

Studying the Psalms

A. Psalm 124—A Psalm of Gratitude for National Deliverance

Read **Psalm 124.** It might be interesting to read the psalm with the leader reading **verse 1,** the group responding with **verses 2–5,** the leader reading **verses 6–7,** and the group responding with **verse 8.**

Israel had experienced a recent deliverance. Now the psalmist invites them to express their gratitude. In **Psalm 107** he encouraged the people thus: "Let the redeemed of the Lord say this—those He redeemed from the hand of the foe" **(v. 2). Psalm 106** invites the people to say, "Amen! Praise the Lord" **(v. 48).** In **Psalm 124** we find another admonition to the people, "Let Israel say."

1. What are they to say? Put it in your own words **(vv. 2–5).**

2. In three word pictures the psalmist describes what would have happened if the Lord had not delivered them. List them:

(v. 3)

(vv. 4–5)

(vv. 6–7)

Now take each word picture and try to interpret its original setting. Then think of a situation today, individually or nationally, that would be similar.

3. Compare the help of the Lord here with that expressed in **Psalm 121.**

4. The psalmist talks about the Lord being on their side. Indeed, He had saved Israel from the enemy. In our world today can we, as citizens, claim that God is on the side of our country? Explain your answer. Perhaps a better question might be "Are we on the Lord's side?"

B. Psalm 67—An Expression of Thanksgiving

When we think of our nation, there are many reasons for thanking God, who continually gives us much more than we deserve. Isaiah warned the Israelites about the mockery of national-religious festivals. They were a sinful nation and estranged from God. (See **Isaiah 1.**) God was severe with them and in essence said, "I despise your yearly celebrations." Read **Isaiah 29:13–15.** Here God seems to say, "You use nice-sounding phrases about honoring Me, but your hearts are not Mine."

An example of true thanksgiving is expressed in **Psalm 67.**

1. The last verses are the key to understanding this psalm. What are the causes for rejoicing **(vv. 6–7)?** What response should this blessing create in us **(v. 7)?**

2. The word *may*, although not a command, still comes as a suggestion regarding a course of action. What is suggested by each phrase **(vv. 3–5)?**

3. God's goodness to Israel reveals Him to other nations. What can other nations observe **(vv. 2, 4, 6)?**

4. **Verse 1** is similar to the wording of the benediction with which Aaron was to bless the people of Israel. Compare with **Numbers 6:22–27.** What do the words "Make His face shine upon you" mean?

More Understanding

1. **Psalm 124** is one of the psalms that is titled "A song of ascents." Read Psalms **120–134.** Use a commentary or Bible dictionary to discover what is meant by "songs of ascents" and how they were used.

2. What other psalms can you find that deal with the nation or with thanksgiving for freedom and deliverance?

3. The story of Esther pictures in a vivid way God's deliverance of the Jewish people. Read the book of **Esther** in the light of this psalm to give you a sense of the magnitude of Israel's deliverance.

For Further Discussion

1. "In God we trust" is on all U.S. money. What do these words mean?

2. Below are the reasons given for the fall of the Roman Empire, according to Edward Gibbon in *Decline and Fall of the Roman Empire.* Discuss each one to see the danger of your country being defeated by these same enemies from within:

a. The rapid increase of divorce; the undermining of the dignity and sanctity of the home, which is the basis of human society;

b. Higher and higher taxes and the spending of public money for free board and circuses for the populace;

c. The mad craze for pleasure; sports becoming more exciting and more brutal every year;

d. The building of gigantic armaments when the real enemy was within—the decadence of the people;

e. The decay of religion: faith fading into mere form, losing touch with life and becoming impotent to guide people.

3. U.S. President John F. Kennedy once quoted the following statement, which has become famous: "Ask not what your country can do for you; ask what you can do for your country." Discuss what you can do for your country.

4. A Christian is to be in the world as light and as salt. (See **Isaiah 49:6; Matthew 5:14–16; Ephesians 5:8; Matthew 5:13.**) For this reason ought we not to involve ourselves in politics? What are you doing to be well informed and concerned about your national elections and about race relations?

5. Historically, what have the citizens of your country experienced that should generate a real spirit of thankfulness to God? In what way have Christians been a light and a salt in your country's history?

6. What important thought did these psalms leave with you?

Lesson 8

God Speaks
about Deliverance
from Trouble
(Psalm 107)

Aims

To be assured that God delivers from trouble.

To thank God when we experience such deliverance and to tell others about it.

Purpose

Often we hear people say, "The Bible says, 'God helps those who help themselves.'" Nowhere in the Bible is there such a statement. On the other hand, the Bible has much to say about those who cried to the Lord in their helplessness and *He helped them.*

Many times we hear the expression "They were at their wits' end." Hardly anyone knows that this expression *is* from the Bible. In fact, it occurs in **verse 27** of this psalm.

Studying the Psalm

Read **Psalm 107,** noting the four kinds of distress in **verses 4–9, 10–16, 17–22, 23–32.** The psalm begins and ends with references to the goodness of God.

A. Give Thanks (vv. 1–3)

1. The psalm begins with a call to thanksgiving. For what reasons can we thank God?

2. The psalmist calls God's people "the redeemed of the Lord." From what did He redeem them **(v. 2)**? (See also **Isaiah 62:12.**)

3. The redeemed of the Lord are to "say this." What are they to say?

B. Deliverance of Lost Travelers (vv. 4–9)

1. What were the troubles these people experienced? Who might they have been? (See **Numbers 10:11–11:32.**)

2. What did they do in their distress?

3. What did God do?

4. What is the psalmist's admonition?

5. Although traveling in the desert may not be a common experience for many of us, we all may encounter problems or hazards in travel. Try to find a modern counterpart in **verses 4–9** for this distress. How might help come?

C. Deliverance from Imprisonment (vv. 10–16)

1. What were the troubles experienced in these verses? Who might these prisoners have been? (See **Deuteronomy 26:5–11.**) Note that God healed through His Word. (Compare with **Mark 2:5–12; Isaiah 55:11.**)

2. Note again what the prisoners did, what God did, and what the psalmist's admonition is.

3. We may not know what it is to live behind prison walls, but each of us has experienced feelings of imprisonment from time to time, whether it be by the four walls of home where we are caught with children, or whether it be limitations imposed upon us by a dominating habit (which may be as serious as drug addiction or as seemingly innocent as not getting enough sleep). Read again **verses 11–16** and describe some feeling of "imprisonment" you may have had and the deliverance you experienced. How did release come?

D. Deliverance from Sickness (vv. 17–22)

1. What were the troubles of these people?

2. Most of us have had some experience with healing after illness. We may or may not have had any thought of God in this healing. Read again **verses 17–22.** Can you identify this with some experience you have had? How did healing come?

E. Deliverance from Storms (vv. 23–32)

1. What were the troubles described in this section? Compare the description of the storm with that recorded in **Mark 4:35–41.**

2. Note again what the seafarers did, what God did, and what the admonitions are.

3. Have you ever experienced a storm at sea or heard someone tell of such an experience? Read again **verses 23–32** and see if you can translate this experience into some "storm of life" you have had. How did your deliverance come?

4. In the Lord's Prayer we pray, "Deliver us from evil." Does God answer this prayer by keeping us from all evil or by helping us in our trouble? Or does He do both? How?

F. Meditation on God's Providence (vv. 33–43)

1. Read **verses 1–3** and **33–43,** noting God's goodness. Why is it good to give thanks? For what blessings can you thank God?

2. How does the Lord deal with the wicked?

3. How does He deal with the upright?

4. What will the wise do?

5. What important thought did this psalm leave with you?

More Understanding

1. If you have a commentary on **Psalms,** read what it says about **Psalm 107.**

2. Glance through the psalms to find others that have admonitions to give thanks to God for His providence and deliverance.

3. Study **Psalm 136,** noting all the things the psalmist enumerates for which to give thanks. Why do you think he repeats the words "give thanks" and "His love endures forever"? What is a litany?

4. The following comparisons may enrich the understanding of this psalm:

Verse 22—Hebrews 13:15; Psalm 116:17

Verse 33—Isaiah 42:15; 50:2

Verse 35—Isaiah 41:18

Verse 40—Job 12:21–24

Verse 42—Job 22:19

Lesson 9

God Speaks about Hatred of Evildoers (Psalms 137 and 139)

Aims

To understand why the psalmists felt free to ask God to act against wicked persons who defied Him.

To see the difference between personal resentment and the hatred of forces that oppose God.

To see that Christians can love and forgive even their enemies because of Jesus.

Purpose

A number of wonderful psalms are "spoiled" for us because in them we find verses that seem so wrong in their intent. They are called "imprecatory psalms." To *imprecate* means "to pray evil or misfortune on others." We hesitate to read these psalms in group meetings because these sections offend us. They seem to say the opposite of what we are taught in the Sermon on the Mount. We need help to understand the spirit in which such shocking statements were made. We shall look at two imprecatory sections (**Psalm 137:8–9; 139:19–22**).

When **Psalm 137** was written, the psalmist and many of the Israelites had been in captivity. The Babylonians were the enemies who had tormented them.

Because the psalmist thought of himself and his people as God's people, he also thought of his enemies as God's enemies because he was living in a covenant relationship with God. The psalmist was on God's side; therefore, his enemies were God's enemies. For the same reason God's enemies were also his enemies.

The psalmist's faith in the Lord's righteous government of the world demanded that the Lord act in some effective way against His enemies. This the psalmist dared to pray for.

Studying the Psalms

A. Psalm 137: A Psalm of Love and Hate

Read **Psalm 137,** noting the two sections: love **(vv. 1–6)** and hate **(vv. 7–9).**

Love **(vv. 1–6)**

1. In what situation had the Israelites been? (Read **2 Kings 25:1–12** for details.)

2. In what emotional state were they as they remembered Jerusalem and the songs of Zion **(vv. 3–6)?**

3. Rethink the situation in which the Israelites had found themselves in Babylon. Share what you have discovered in your study about the Babylonian captivity. Try to enter into the conflicting emotions the people experienced. How would you react if you were imprisoned and being tortured and were forced to sing "Alas! and Did My Savior Bleed" for the amusement of your atheistic tormentors? Even in our modern times people have had similar experiences in concentration camps. Share any information you might have about such treatment.

Hate (**vv. 7–9**)

4. When the psalmist remembered Jerusalem, he also was reminded of the Edomites, who rejoiced in the devastation of the city. What was his reaction to them and his prayer?

5. The psalmist's language seems too severe for us. It seems to be in contradiction to Christian teachings. On the other hand, is it not true that too often we are silent and passive toward those who bring evil into our midst?

6. When have you been angry enough about those who ruin our youth with drugs, liquor, prostitution, or pornography to talk to God about it—to ask Him to break their power of evil, or to do something about it?

7. When have you been angry enough about racial inequality to take sides, make a protest, or do something to change it? What kind of action have you or your group taken?

B. Psalm 139: A Wise Man's Prayer

Read **Psalm 139,** noting these divisions: the prayer of a believing heart (**vv. 1–12**), we are wonderfully made (**vv. 13–18**), hatred for the wicked

(vv. 19–24). Although we are especially interested in this last section in this study of imprecatory psalms, it is very fitting that we see hatred for evil in the perspective of the whole Christian life.

He lives close to God **(vv. 1–18)**

1. The psalmist is overawed by the fact that God knows so much about him. What items of knowledge does he list **(vv. 1–6)?**

2. The psalmist finds it hard to escape from such a knowing God. List the "if" suppositions he thinks through **(vv. 7–12).**

3. How does he describe God's knowledge of his prenatal state **(vv. 13–18)?**

He can't bear the thought of people who defy God **(vv. 19–24).**

4. What does the psalmist ask God to do to His enemies **(vv. 19–22)?** How does our attitude toward evil and enemies (personal ones or enemies of God) differ from the attitude of those living in Old Testament times? How do you account for this difference?

5. The psalmist makes God's enemies his enemies. What strong feeling does he repeat (vv. 21–22)? Was it hostility for a personal hurt that he felt, or what was it?

6. As you read his prayer (vv. 23–24), do you think he feels guilty for hating? Give your reasons. It is difficult not to let our hatred of evil become a personal resentment against the evil. Read **Romans 12:9–21** and discuss what light it gives on hatred of evil and how we are to overcome evil because we belong to Christ Jesus. How did He reach out to us when we were *His* enemies? (See **Romans 5:10.**)

C. Deliverance from Evildoers, Then and Now

1. How do our petitions in the Lord's Prayer differ from the way the psalmist calls down God's judgment upon evildoers? We pray, "Deliver us from evil." Evil is done by evildoers. What are we asking God to do in the Lord's Prayer? Did you feel that the psalmist's prayer in **Psalm 139:23–24** was his way of questioning the rightness of his feeling of hatred toward the evildoers? Is there a place for hatred in a Christian's life?

2. What important thought did this psalm leave with you?

More Understanding

1. In **Psalm 137** we see God's people weeping because of calamity. In **Psalm 126** we see the same people back in Jerusalem, full of gratitude.

Tears have been changed into shouts of joy for freedom, prosperity, and well-being. Read **Psalm 126** and try to understand the people's feeling of joy.

2. Look on a map to see how far Babylon (on the Euphrates River) is from Jerusalem. It will help you to realize how strange the people of Israel must have felt in this heathen land. Also locate Edom, the nation that gloated over the fact that Jerusalem was to be razed. **2 Kings 25:1–12** tells the story of the captivity. Read also **Isaiah 46–47** to see the judgment on Babylon.

3. Having read how the psalmist prayed to God about enemies, read in **Acts 4:29–31** how the early Christians prayed about the enemies of the Gospel. Read the Sermon on the Mount **(Matthew 5–7)** and commentaries, if possible, to see the different attitudes Christians are expected to have toward their enemies and the enemies of God.

Lesson 10

God Speaks about Doubt (Psalm 73)

Aim

To learn how to overcome doubt.

Purpose

Why do the wicked prosper? Why do Christians suffer? This is an age-old question that has troubled humankind in each generation.

There are many "pat answers" that people give freely, but they come too easily and will not do. They give small comfort to those who suffer. The most common ones are that (1) suffering is the consequence of sin; (2) it is the will of God; (3) suffering comes to test us.

The Bible does not fully explain suffering, but points the way toward overcoming it—how to come through it "better," not "bitter." It points to the source of power to *transform* tragedy into triumph. **Psalm 73** gives us help in this direction.

The psalmist Asaph gives us an account of his experience with envy and doubt over the perplexing problem of the prosperity of the wicked and the suffering of the righteous. He had been so frustrated and deeply troubled that he begins the psalm with the idea "You wouldn't think it sometimes, but God really is good to His people."

Studying the Psalm

Read **Psalm 73** and notice the following divisions:
Verses 1–3—the problem
Verses 4–16—the struggle
Verses 17–28—the victory

A. God Is Good (vv. 1–3)

Read the problem as stated in **verses 1–3.** This psalm is typical of Hebrew poetry. It begins with a generalization or a summary statement, which is really the conclusion, and then goes on to elaborate on the problem. What is the truth from which the psalmist deviates and to which he returns in victory? Compare **verses 1** and **28.** But what happened to his confidence in this truth?

1. To whom is God good?

2. There was a time when Asaph doubted this. What was the reason for his doubts?

3. When you have seen how some people seem to prosper in spite of questionable ethics, have you ever questioned the value of faith in God? Does this say anything to us about our modern sense of values?

B. The Prosperity of the Wicked (vv. 4–9)

In his disappointment with God's rule, the psalmist cannot "see straight." He was very confused by the prosperity of the wicked.

1. How does he describe the status of the wicked?

2. What is the attitude of the wicked to others **(vv. 8–9)?**

3. Take each description of the wicked in these verses and translate it into a description of people you know today. How do they seem to draw people after them?

C. People Are Led Astray by the Example of the Wicked (vv. 10–12)
1. How do people react toward the wicked?

2. How does Asaph further describe the life of the wicked **(v. 12)?**

3. Have you ever felt as the psalmist did in these verses? Do you wonder why you have lived a good life and all the rewards seem to be given to others?

D. The Psalmist Is Frustrated (vv. 13–16)
1. Why does he feel his godly life was in vain?

2. In **verse 15** the psalmist says that although he had these doubts he kept them to himself. When is it wise not to talk about your doubts to others?

3. What was it that troubled Asaph **(v. 16)?**

E. Turning Point (v. 17)

1. The word *till* indicates the turning point in the psalmist's dilemma. He went from doubt to faith, from bitterness to strength. In fact, the whole psalm divides into two parts: **(a)** confusion until **(vv. 1–16)** and **(2)** understanding thereafter **(vv. 17–28).**

Where was he when the solution came to him?

2. In this instance the psalmist found that struggling with the situation was tiresome work, but he finally found his victory in God's house. Then his perspectives became clear, and he was able to see things from an eternal point of view. If you are struggling with doubts at the present time, what could you learn from this experience of the psalmist that would help you?

F. The End of the Wicked (vv. 18–20)

What was the actual situation with the wicked?

G. The Difference in Asaph (vv. 21–26)

1. Looking back on it, how does Asaph describe his period of doubt **(vv. 21–22)?**

2. The psalmist is pretty hard on himself in **verses 21–22** as he

describes the foolishness of his doubt. Has life ever made you bitter to this extent?

3. With the return of faith, what does Asaph realize **(vv. 23–24)?**

4. In spite of this wandering into doubt and envy and forgetting the goodness of God, what does Asaph in **verses 23–26** realize about God's relationship to him? God never abandons us. Faithlessness is always on our side. In your experience, what are some things that have forced you to quit looking at others and look at God? Is the Christian's highest good in life to have freedom from all troubles? An Arab proverb says, "All sunshine makes the desert." How is this true in human life? What comfort and consolation do you receive from **verses 25–26?**

H. A Contrast (vv. 27–28)
1. What will happen to those far from God?

2. What is the confession of one who is near God?

3. What does he have to tell?

4. What important thought did this psalm leave with you?

More Understanding

1. What has Asaph been trying to say? Surely there will have been many statements that puzzled you as you studied this psalm. Defining words, comparing translations, and looking up cross-references will give you greater insights.

2. Seek to understand the two kinds of people mentioned. Note Christ's promise to the "pure in heart" in **Matthew 5:8.** (Also read **Psalm 84:11; 25:8;** and **24:4–5.**) Contrast what Asaph said about the "wicked" in **verses 4–9** and **18–20.**

3. Look up the meaning of *sanctuary* in the dictionary. (Note **Ezekiel 11:16; Psalm 63:2; 20:2; 96:6; 150:1.**)

4. Study **Psalm 37** and compare with **Psalm 73.**

Lesson 11

God Speaks about Thanksgiving (Psalm 92)

Aims

To learn what can be included in a prayer of thanksgiving.
To be reminded that it is good to give thanks to God.

Purpose

As we approach this psalm, let us give some thought to the question "Is our Thanksgiving Day a holiday or a holy day?" This depends upon what we do with it. If it is only a time away from the job, a time for family gatherings and perhaps a football game, then it is certainly a holiday—a time to make merry. If it is kept by us as individuals and families and the congregation as a day to give thanks to God, then it is also a holy day. At the same time it can also be a holiday for us in that we have freedom from labor and leisure for recreation.

It is also a festival, a day of celebrating, of being joyous. In the Old Testament, God used religious feasts as a means of teaching the young and reminding the adults of His great works. For instance, the Passover was the covenant feast of Israel. Traditionally, at the festive table at a certain place in the ritual, a son would ask his father, "Why do we keep this feast?" Then the father would tell the story of God's deliverance of Israel from Egyptian bondage.

Our Thanksgiving Day family observance should also be a time of instruction and reminder as we talk about the origin of this celebration and the great works of God for which we give thanks and praise, especially the gift of His Son Jesus. This does not just happen. We need to plan for it and encourage it. We need to know Scripture passages, which we will share at the festive table. This psalm is one such gem. Let us look at it closely.

Psalm 92 is a song for the Sabbath. God Himself said, "Observe the Sabbath day by keeping it holy, as the Lord your God has commanded you . . . . Remember that you were slaves in Egypt and that the Lord your God brought you out of there with a mighty hand and an outstretched arm. Therefore the Lord your God has commanded you to observe the Sabbath day" **(Deuteronomy 5:12, 15).**

We remember that we were slaves to sin and that the Lord has brought us out of its bondage through faith in Christ Jesus. We have an even greater cause for praise.

Studying the Psalm

A. It Is Good to Praise the Lord (vv. 1–4)

1. What response to God's goodness does the psalmist suggest in **verses 1–2?**

2. What is another name the psalmist gives to the Lord **(v. 1)?** What does this tell us about God? (See also **Genesis 14:18–20; Psalm 7:10, 17.)**

3. When are we to proclaim the Lord's love **(v. 2)?** How are we to proclaim it **(v. 3)?** Why are we to proclaim it **(v. 4)?**

B. The Greatness of God's Works (vv. 5–11)

1. Of what two things does the psalmist stand in awe **(v. 5)?** (See also **Romans 11:33** and **Isaiah 55:8.)** What are some of the works of God that arouse a spirit of thanksgiving and praise in us?

2. From whom is the meaning of God's works and thoughts hidden (**v. 6**)? When the psalmist says that senseless men and fools cannot understand these things, he is referring to those who are spiritually senseless and foolish. How does the Spirit work to take away our senselessness and foolishness? Is it not spiritually senseless and foolish to be unaware of the things for which we ought to be grateful, and to neglect to give thanks on Thanksgiving Day or any other day?

3. What is the fate of the Lord's enemies (**vv. 7–9**)?

4. What is the meaning behind the picture language in **verse 10?**

5. What is the fate of the psalmist's enemies (**v. 11**)?

C. Prosperity of the Righteous (vv. 12–15)
Read **verses 12–15** to see a contrasting picture of the righteous.
1. What do you think is meant by the two figures used to describe the righteous in **verse 12?**

2. How are the characteristics of these trees symbolic of the Christian?

3. What does it mean that the righteous are "planted in the house of the Lord"?

4. How is their flourishing described **(v. 14)?** Explain this in your own words.

5. **Verses 14–15** present a tremendous picture of the fruitfulness of the righteous. What has this to do with thanksgiving and praise? What do you have for which to be thankful?

6. What do we learn about the Lord in **verse 15** for which to be thankful?

More Understanding

1. Go through the psalms and note how often gratitude to God is expressed. Note especially the following psalms: **136; 107; 103; 118.** You may also want to study psalms **18; 30; 32; 34; 40; 41; 66; 124; 129; 138.**

2. Glancing through these psalms again, note references to the love of God. This concept of God's unwavering faithfulness is basic to a spirit of thanksgiving and praise.

3. Using a concordance, commentary, and/or Bible dictionary, make a study of "Sabbath," "house of the Lord," "upright," "righteous," and "wicked."

Lesson 12

God Speaks When I Think of the Passing of Time (Psalm 90)

Aims

To see the brevity of our existence.
To appreciate God's timelessness.
To become wise stewards of time.

Purpose

Every December the calendar runs out, and we bid farewell to another year. Year's end is always a time of reckoning, the end of fiscal accounting, the time for final reports. At that time of year we sense anew how responsible we are for the use of our life, our time, our possessions, our talents. It is a time to face our failures and sins and a time to seek forgiveness. It is a time to count our blessings and to give thanks. But it is also a time to anticipate the year ahead. What will it bring? What will we bring to it? Fear and hope go hand in hand as our companions, but courage comes as we look into the face of God and say:

Yesterday He helped;
Today He did the same.
How long will this continue?
Forever! Praise His name!

Studying the Psalm

A. Human Life Is Short; God Is Eternal (vv. 1–6)

Read the entire psalm, noting the references to time and eternity. This psalm is suggested for use at the end of the year or at a funeral. Discuss the appropriateness for these occasions. It may be interesting to note that while this psalm speaks of the eternal God, no thought is given to eternal life for humans.

This psalm is attributed to Moses. The opening sentence, which addresses God as the dwelling place of people in all generations, corresponds exactly in thought and language to the memorable sentence in the great hymn of praise Moses sang just before his death. (See **Deuteronomy 33:27.**)

1. The inscription gives Moses a special title. What is he called? (See **Joshua 14:6** for the source of this title.)

2. How far back does Moses trace God's existence **(vv. 1–2)?**

3. These first verses deal with God's eternity and humankind's transitoriness. Discuss some of God's attributes as revealed here. Contrast these with the attributes of humans. As we think of the shortness of human life and its apparent insignificance, what does **Psalm 8:3–8** tell us?

4. What does it mean to turn men back to dust **(v. 3)?** (See **Genesis 2:7; 3:19.**)

5. Even a thousand years are a very small thing to God. To what two things are a thousand years compared **(v. 4)?** (See also **2 Peter 3:8** for similarity.) What does the psalmist mean to say by this?

6. What word pictures does Moses use for the brevity of human existence (**vv. 5–6**)?

B. God's Displeasure with Sin (vv. 7–12)

Read **verses 7–12**. Note the element of time and the shortness of life.

1. God's displeasure with sin is Moses' explanation for human mortality. What two words does he use to describe God's displeasure (**v. 7**)?

2. What two things does God see in human beings (**v. 8**)?

3. What is the end of human life like (**v. 9**)?

4. Even at its best, human life is short. Of what two ingredients is it full (**v. 10**)?

5. **Verse 11** indicates the tendency of people to ignore the wrath of God. What attitude ought Christians have toward life? (See also **Deuteronomy 32:29.** Put this in your own words.)

6. What great lesson, summarized in **verse 12,** is to be learned from this section? How does this lesson apply to us in our daily living, and what difference would it make in using our time wisely?

C. A Prayer for God's Forgiveness and Favor (vv. 13–17)

Read **verses 13–17.** Note particularly what the psalmist is asking God to do. It might be interesting to read this section one verse at a time and put it into common language to see exactly what it says.

1. In the question asked of God in **verses 13–14,** what do the people really want?

2. For how much gladness do they ask **(v. 15)?**

3. Giving joy in proportion to evil is the deed of God they ask for. To whom shall this deed be shown **(v. 16)?**

4. With what twofold prayer does Moses close his psalm **(v. 17)?**

5. Jot a note on your calendar to reread this psalm on December 31. As you look back over the year, formulate a prayer that will give expression to your particular needs. Look backward over the past year or few years, contemplate how quickly time goes, and evaluate what things could well have been left undone and what things were of eternal value. Then look ahead and determine how you would pray so your work could be "established" —

that is, be of some eternal significance. What is really enduring? Instead of making resolutions for the new year, write a prayer to God, voicing your concern in this regard.

6. What important thought did this psalm leave with you?

More Understanding

1. Make a list of all the attributes of God mentioned in **Psalm 90.** Make another list of His acts.

2. In a dictionary look up the meaning of the words *eternal* and *transitory.* What does this add to your understanding of the difference between God and human beings?

3. Read **Psalm 8** and compare the significance of humans in this psalm and in **Psalm 90.**

4. Examine the hymn "Our God, Our Help in Ages Past" and compare it with the text of **Psalm 90.**

PSALMS
Conversations with God

Leaders Notes

Leaders Notes

Preparing to Teach Psalms

Aims of the Study

Perhaps no other portion of the Scriptures is so well known and yet so little understood as the book of **Psalms.** Most people who know anything about the Bible know a few "literary gems" from the psalms. But we who are not satisfied with a few oft-quoted verses are invited to a full meal, a banquet. We are invited to sit down at the table and enjoy the spiritual food found in **Psalms.**

Of course, it will be possible to study only a few of the 150 psalms. However, we shall endeavor to get acquainted with some of the various types of psalms, such as psalms of praise, of thanksgiving, of trust, and of repentance; also messianic psalms and imprecatory psalms. (To imprecate means to pray for evil or misfortune upon an enemy.)

In this study it is hoped that the participants will:

1. Be able to read any psalm and know how to discover its message.

2. Learn how to use the psalmists' words to express their own moods, needs, or joys; how to praise and thank God; how to express grief, frustration, and suffering; how to affirm trust-thoughts.

3. Memorize favorite passages for their own spiritual growth and for the purpose of sharing them with others.

4. Enrich their understanding of God. The psalmists give many descriptions of God and His qualities.

5. See the psalms through the light of the Gospel of Christ and apply that Good News to their lives.

6. Learn how to pray.

7. Learn from the psalms how to face life with confidence and courage.

General Instructions

To you has been given a great privilege and a great responsibility. As you study and prepare, you will be greatly blessed, and you will find it a privilege to help others grow in faith as you lead them in Bible study.

Your first reaction may be one of inadequacy and hesitation. In fact, you may wonder why you were chosen to lead when you don't know all the answers and when you may not know your Bible any better than the rest. In this you may be quite correct, but keep in mind that you are not asked to be a *lecturer* or to give all the answers. You are only asked to *lead* the group in a *joint discovery* of truth.

These Leaders Notes will give definite suggestions as to what your duties are—what to do and what not to do. Following these closely will help you do a good job.

The Role of the Leader

1. *Your first role as a leader is to be the encourager.*

The group will expect you to radiate enthusiasm and readiness to lead. Your enthusiasm will then be caught, and the participants will want to enter into this great experience with you.

The group will look to you to make them feel comfortable, at ease, informal. You will want to help participants experience Christian love and fellowship, to encourage neighborliness and friendships.

The group will expect you to challenge them to join in discussions, to search Scripture together, to ask and answer questions during class time, and to do any extra work suggested in each lesson.

2. *Your second role as a leader is to be the enabler.*

Good group work requires that the place of meeting be ready and attractive, not too large and not too small, and above all, that it be arranged so that informal discussion is possible.

The leader should stress the importance of study group members bringing their own Bibles and a pen or pencil to mark words and verses with special meaning to them.

Plan a time schedule. Include time for devotions, your introduction, and sharing facts from the lesson. Some time should be used for sharing what the words and expressions mean. But perhaps most of the time available should be devoted to applying the message to life's situations. You may not have time to cover everything. Therefore you must choose.

As the leader, guide the discussion, being careful not to talk too much. Rather, encourage participation by all. If the discussion goes too far afield, bring the group back to the main topic. Don't let the group spend too much time on one little issue. Keep the lesson moving!

Be sensitive to the feelings of the shy member who never enters the discussion and seems ill at ease. Be careful not to put a member "on the spot." If an answer is inadequate, "save the day" by thanking the person for his or her contribution and then tactfully adding a bit of information to strengthen or correct the answer.

Your most difficult task as leader, perhaps, will be to curb the member who monopolizes the discussion. Patience, love, and tactful firmness will be required.

3. *Your third role as a leader is to be an intercessor.*

Prayer is the most important preparation for Bible study. We need to call on the Holy Spirit, who inspired the Word of God, to interpret it to us and to help us understand it. As the leader, you will want to ask for wisdom and understanding for yourself and for each member of the group according to his or her needs and trials. You should anticipate the group meeting by asking for God's power. At the meeting you should stress prayer and ask each member to be faithful in intercession.

Preparation of the Lesson

In **Ps. 119:17–18** the psalmist prayed, "Do good to Your servant, and I will live; I will obey Your word. Open my eyes that I may see wonderful things in Your law." To be able to see wonderful things, the psalmist needed eyes that were opened by the Lord. This suggests how we, too—leaders and group members—must begin.

1. Find a quiet, comfortable place where you will be as undisturbed as possible.

2. Have a dictionary, several translations of the Bible, and a concordance available, if possible. If you own a commentary on the Psalms, it should also be within reach.

3. Close your eyes, relax your body and mind, and talk to your heavenly Father. Thank Him for the privilege that is yours to lead this study. Admit your inadequacy for the job. Ask Him to help you and empower you with His Holy Spirit. Ask Him to motivate you to love all.

4. Think of the members of your group and ask God to help them in whatever problems, burdens, griefs, suffering, and frustrations they may face. Above all, ask God to increase the hunger for Him so that all will desire the Word, be eager to learn at the meeting, and be eager to do any suggested homework.

5. Read the whole psalm assigned for the meeting. Remember that it is the faith of the Old Testament believers expressed in poetry. As you read, do so with purpose. Look for something definite, as well as the general mood of the psalm. Look for statements of what God is like and how He deals with people. Look for God's promises, especially the Good News of salvation to come through His Son, Jesus. Also look for how the psalmist felt, what troubles and joys he faced, how he talked with God, what help came to him. You will see interesting comparisons, contrasts, word pic-

tures, and parallelisms. (A parallelism is composed of two or more sentences that mean the same thing but are expressed with different words. Or a parallelism may be two contrasting ideas or the development of a thought.)

6. Look up cross-references in the Bible. Remember that one part of the Bible throws light on another part. Watch especially for references to God's promise of salvation, which was fulfilled by Jesus' death on the cross and resurrection to eternal life.

7. Read the psalm in various translations.

8. Study the lesson by using the Bible Study Guide. Carefully write out all answers.

9. Memorize one or several favorite passages.

10. Aware of any special needs in your group, try to anticipate how the message of this psalm might help the participants. For instance, how would this psalm help the woman whose husband is a skeptic and has no use for God? or the man who recently lost a loved one in death? etc.

11. When you have studied the psalm, go over your notes again and simplify them. Too many notes are confusing. Underline the most important points you hope will be discussed. You may want to have a few other good discussion questions ready in case they are needed. Questions that cannot be answered with yes or no but with an opinion will stimulate sharing of ideas.

12. Having done this detail, close your eyes and see the psalm as a whole. Note how its lesson may be applied to your daily life. Try to put into one sentence what you have learned. For example, "God takes care of me; I need not fear."

13. Now you are ready to go over the section "Introduction to the Lesson" in the lesson. Jot down your plan of procedure. You may not follow it exactly in order to be flexible to the needs of the group.

14. Again turn to God, asking Him to make this study meaningful. Then relax and trust Him.

Lesson 1

God Speaks to Assure Me of His Existence
(Psalm 19)

Aims

To know God in the world He created, in His Word, and through experiences with Him.

To gain assurance that God will sustain us through our life.

Leader's Personal Preparation

1. If possible, do your planning for the meeting and your Bible study very early so that as the days go by, the Holy Spirit can bring truths to your mind and can tie into a total picture what you hear, read, experience, and pray about. Give the psalm time to grip you and to unfold for you.

2. Read the instructions for the leader at the beginning of this manual. *Do not omit this.* This is very important each time you prepare.

3. Do the lesson in the Study Guide before class time to familiarize yourself with it.

4. Carefully read the introduction and Bible study helps for this lesson in this guide. Do not omit this. Make notes for yourself as you go along.

5. Through the material offered in this guide, you can gain a background for discussion and questions that will help you *lead* wisely. Remember that you are not to be the *answer-giver*, but you are to help the group *discover* the answers together.

Introduction to the Lesson

If possible, have a picture display of beautiful nature scenes.

1. *Begin with devotions.*

Read the theme verse **(Col. 3:16).** Help the group see these parts of the theme verse: (a) living in the Word, (b) teaching and admonishing, (c) praising God in song, and (d) thanking God in our hearts and lives. Pray that the Holy Spirit might strengthen them as they study God's Word so that they might live in the Word, teach and admonish, and praise and give thanks to God.

2. *Explain your role as a leader and the role of the group.*

Explain that you are not the question-answerer, but will help the group have fun discovering and sharing insights. It is important that you emphasize the value of each member's contributions to the class session. Especially urge members to preread the psalm and bring to class any observations and questions they may have.

3. *Give the background of the book* of Psalms.

Ask participants to share what they know about the background and history of the psalms and their use. Here are a few facts to share:

a. The book of Psalms, as we know it, was not *made*—it *grew*, just as our hymnals were not made but grew as person after person through the centuries expressed deep spiritual experiences in poetic form. Some of the hymn writers wrote hundreds of years ago; some are living today.

b. Christ loved the psalms. Raised as a Jewish boy, He was nourished on the psalms of His people. The psalms were read and sung in His home. He heard them in the synagogue. Later, at His Baptism, His vocation as Messiah was affirmed with **Ps. 2:7,** "You are My Son." In the night in which He was betrayed, after Jesus instituted the Last Supper, He and the eleven sang a hymn before going to the Mount of Olives **(Matt. 26:30).** In all likelihood, this hymn was the Hallel **(Psalm 113–118),** a regular part of the Passover ritual. In a discussion with the Sadducees **(Luke 20:27–40),** Jesus quoted **Psalm 110** to show that He was the Messiah sent by God. On the cross, when His agony was greatest, Jesus used the words of David **(Ps. 22:1)** to express the horror of forsakenness. On Easter evening, when Jesus startled the eleven by His sudden appearance, He declared that everything written about Him in the psalms must be fulfilled **(Luke 24:44).**

c. Christ's followers loved the psalms too. Peter quoted from Psalms in his great Pentecost sermon **(Acts 2:25–35).** Paul encourages us to use them **(Eph. 5:19).** James advises us to use them to express a happy heart **(James 5:13).**

May we, too, learn to love them. This will not come suddenly, but as the result of prayerful reading and faithful study of the psalms.

d. It is not known who the author of every psalm was. In fact, 34 psalms are called "orphans" by the Jews because their authors are unknown. The titles or short inscriptions found at the beginning of many psalms were not part of the sacred text. They were added later and are meant to instruct us. Following are some of the authors and the number of psalms they are thought to have written: 73 by David; 12 by Asaph; 11 in a collection of the sons of Korah (a Levitical musical guild); 2 by Solomon; 1 by Moses; 1 by a Levite named Ethan.

e. The psalms are Hebrew poetry. Hebrew poetry is not dependent on meter or rhyme as our poetry often is. Its construction depends upon *rhythm of thought* and *balance of sentences*. For instance, in two or more lines the subject matter corresponds:

> Enter His gates with thanksgiving
> and His courts with praise.

These two lines mean practically the same thing. Sometimes the second line strengthens the first by contrast, connected with the word *but*.

> For the Lord watches over the way of the righteous,
> but the way of the wicked will perish.

These are called *parallelisms*. There are many parallelisms in the psalms, and this is one observation to make in each study. Other characteristics to watch for are word pictures, contrasts, repetitions, questions, descriptions of God and His qualities, and the moods of the writers.

f. The word *Selah* is found 71 times in the psalms. Its meaning and use are uncertain. It usually is regarded as a musical interlude. When a psalm is read aloud, this word is not spoken.

4. *Encourage group discussion.*

Read together the aims and purpose of the lesson. Answer any questions the group may have about these.

Then read through all of **Psalm 19.** Be sure that the group sees the psalm as a whole before you begin to discuss it in its various parts. You may wish to emphasize the parallelisms by having part of the group read the first part of each verse and the rest of the group read the last part. After this initial reading you may want to have the divisions reread as you discuss each section.

You may wish to ask individuals to share particular information. In this psalm, for instance, if you have someone who is a scientist or is interested in science, you might ask that person to do some pointed thinking for the group on the question relating to natural laws and share some of modern science's understanding of God's creation. Another person might do a little extra study on the meaning of the Torah or the Law in Old Testament times.

Proceed through the discussion suggestions, giving time for members to share their own insights and experiences.

Studying the Psalm

Approach this psalm with your study group members as if your faith in God has been challenged by someone who asks the question "How do you know there is a God?" The psalmist, too, may have wondered about this, for he proceeds to give us three wonderful reasons for this certainty:

A. David Sees God's Hand in Creation (Ps. 19:1–6)

1. He first invites us to look at the *heavens* and the *skies*. Often these

words are used interchangeably. In other words, what David says in line 1 means the same thing as what he says in line 2. This is a parallelism. It is used for emphasis. Keep your eyes open for more such parallelisms. The two verbs are *declare* and *proclaim*.

2. Now the writer shows us four ways in which the message is wonderful:

a. The message that we get from looking at the wonders of creation is like a continued story. During the day everything we see tells us we have a great God. At night the moon and stars tell us the same message. It is unending **(v. 2)**.

b. Although we hear no voice with our ears, yet creation declares the certainty of God's existence **(v. 3)**.

c. Every part of the earth has its special charm that speaks of God's skill in creating. Everywhere in the world, on any continent, in any season of the year, there is beauty that testifies to the Creator **(v. 4)**.

Although we cannot understand the words of people in a foreign land, nature has its own way of communicating God's greatness.

The psalmist now points our attention to a special marvel of creation, the *sun*. The sun makes its daily appearance in the heavens, which are stretched out like a tent **(v. 4)**. (See **Is. 40:22** and **Ps. 104:2.**)

3. The sun is compared to a bridegroom, full of joy, and a champion, strong, ready to run his course **(v. 5)**. The sun's light reveals when and where our God is to be praised **(Ps. 113:3)**.

B. David Sees God in the Word (Ps. 19:7–11)

Suddenly the psalmist drops the subject of God being revealed in creation. Without further introduction, he begins to speak of God in the Word. The transition here is from the revelation of God in the heavens above to the Law within.

1. Notice the style of writing. In this section we see another example of Hebrew poetry—namely, the use of a variety of words, all meaning practically the same thing.

Note that the Word of God is called *law, statutes, precepts, commands, fear of the Lord,* and *ordinances* **(vv. 7–9)**.

Note the various terms qualifying the Scriptures: *perfect, trustworthy, right, radiant, pure,* and *altogether righteous.* The psalmist emphasizes that we can trust the Word of God.

2. In **verses 7–8** we are told what this Word of God can accomplish within us.

a. *Reviving the soul*—When a person who has fainted regains consciousness and a vigorous, healthy condition, we say that he or she was revived. Has the Word of God ever made you very happy after you had been discouraged and felt forsaken? Has the Word assured you of a heavenly Father who loves you and cares for you and sends you His Son as a rescuer from hopelessness? If so, then it has revived your soul. Nature can't do this. Only the Word of God can.

b. *Making wise the simple*—We are all common people without exceptional wisdom. Often we do not know what is best for us. When we study the Word of God, it tells us what is important and what is not good for us. Let us rejoice that every day we can come back to our heavenly Father in prayer and ask for enough wisdom for that day, and that it will be given to us. (See **James 1:5.**)

c. *Giving joy to the heart*—When we feel disgusted with ourselves because we have felt or said something unworthy or have failed to do something good, we are depressed. David, in **Ps. 32:3–4,** described how he felt as he struggled alone with his sinfulness. In **Psalm 51** he described his condition as one of a dirty heart needing washing. In both psalms, David admitted his sin to God and accepted forgiveness. The result was so wonderful that in **Ps. 32:11** he wrote, "Rejoice in the Lord and be glad, you righteous; sing, all you who are upright in heart!" Our hearts will rejoice, too, if we believe the promises of forgiveness, act as if our sins are washed away, and then thank God.

d. *Giving light to the eyes*—In **Ps. 119:105** the psalmist seems to say that as we go through life step by step, the Word of God will throw light on His will for us. Through the Word we will see truths that will help us in our decisions. Preaching on the mount, Jesus told His followers that they would be able to see God in everything, in all their experiences and in the wonders around them **(Matt. 5:8).**

3. The preciousness of the Word **(v. 10)** is described by the words *gold* and *honey.* For emphasis the poet repeats "pure" gold and "honey from the comb." Gold is used because it is recognized as the most precious of metals and highly desired. Honey is the purest of foods and of great value for nutrition.

4. The value of the Word is further emphasized in **verse 11.** It is so valuable because when we keep the Word—that is, live by it—there is great reward, happiness, and usefulness. (See **Ps. 119:9–11.**)

C. David Sees God in a Personal Experience of Forgiveness (Ps. 19:12–14)

We may not be able to convince others of God's existence from nature or from what the Bible tells us. But when we can say, "I know God exists because of what He has done for me, the joy He has given me, the peace I have," then others will sense our certainty.

1. Although David uses the word *forgive* in **verse 12,** in his other great psalm of repentance, **Psalm 51,** he uses the words *blot out, wash, cleanse.* Note the three words *errors, faults,* and *sins.* We can hide these from other people but not from God. Unconfessed and repressed sins bring tension and unhappiness, even physical breakdown. We do not know how often we sin in a day. Therefore, let us ask God to search our hearts and remove all offenses that He finds **(Ps. 139:23–24).** Willful sins are those that we dare to do in overconfidence, even though we know God hates them. David wants to be blameless and innocent, fully forgiven for past sins and held back from repeating them or adding new sins.

2. With a prayer David brings his poem to a close **(v. 14).** The highest praise God can receive is that from a redeemed sinner. This person can sing a song that angels cannot sing, the song of redemption.

3. A forgiven David can speak about God as his "Lord," "Rock," and "Redeemer."

Conclusion

Discuss the questions in the Study Guide. Then close with prayer. For the closing prayer you might distribute slips of paper and have each member write a short prayer regarding the Bible study. Ask three members to volunteer to pray their prayers out loud. Or select a verse from the psalm (for instance, **v. 14**) and use it for your closing prayer.

Lesson 2

God Speaks
When I Am Frightened (Psalm 46)

Aims

To look realistically at the present world situation.

To see our security as children of God in this world.

Leader's Personal Preparation

1. Do the lesson in the Study Guide before class time to familiarize yourself with it.

2. Carefully read the introduction and Bible study helps for this lesson

in this guide. Do not omit this. Make notes for yourself as you go along.

3. Pray for the guidance of the Holy Spirit as you study. Pray for each member of your study group and for God's presence with your group as you study together.

4. To be well prepared for this lesson, take time to list some of the national, international, and world crises you can think of that have brought fear to humankind within the last few years. Also think of the present tragic situations of which you read in the newspapers today.

Introduction to the Lesson

1. *Begin with devotions.*

The group might read together **verse 1** of **Psalm 46,** followed by moments of silence. A suitable hymn would be "A Mighty Fortress Is Our God." This could be read after you explain that Luther received his inspiration for his great hymn from the words of **Psalm 46.**

2. *Explain the inscription.*

Before beginning a book, the reader should always let the author tell of his or her purpose in writing and of what he or she hopes the reader will experience. Before reading a psalm, we should also let the inscription tell us of the author and the purpose. Although the inscription is not part of the original text, it was added later to help us.

a. *For the director of music.* This bit of information suggests that the psalm was set to music and was meant to be sung by a choir in public worship.

b. *Of the Sons of Korah.* This is one of 11 psalms belonging to a collection of sacred pieces either written or gathered by a family or Levitical guild called the Sons of Korah.

c. *According to alamoth.* Here we have a musical term probably meaning soprano voices or a choir of young women. It might also refer to the young women who played tambourines to accompany the singers on the way to the temple.

d. *A song.* This was meant to be sung.

The word *Selah* (which is not to be read) occurs 71 times in the Psalms. Its meaning and use are both uncertain. Some think it is a word of musical direction.

3. *Discuss the psalm.*

a. Before you read the psalm, mention that the psalmist uses two contrasting word pictures to bring his message, "We will not fear," to his readers: the world in commotion in contrast to the "glad" city of God. Read the entire psalm.

b. Reread each section of the psalm and follow this with the discussion suggested. Allow time for sharing of additional insights and understanding by those who have done enrichment study. You may wish to divide into small groups and discuss the three sections before sharing the information with the entire group.

c. Remember that the heart of this psalm is the admonition not to be afraid. Be sure to discuss this basic issue and relate how a Christian can be at peace in the midst of disturbance. Stress the place of prayer in the Christian's life as a means of tapping into God's power.

Studying the Psalm

Every time we look into the Word of God we can learn more about how to pray. Our Christian life is strong or weak, depending on our prayer life. We need to realize that our praying can be selfish and full of doubting. Often it is a mere coaxing of God to give us what we want. Earnestness in prayer increases as we know more about how God deals with people and nations and as we are able to claim His promises. From this psalm we can learn how to pray when we are frightened.

Note the progression of the psalm:

a. In holy confidence the psalmist affirms that we will not fear in times of trouble **(vv. 1–2)**.

b. The psalmist sees commotion in the world **(vv. 2–3)**.

c. In contrast, he sees God's glad city **(vv. 4–7)**.

d. He hears the invitation to see God at work **(vv. 8–9)**.

e. The exalted God speaks: "Be still, and know" **(v. 10)**.

f. The psalmist repeats, "The Lord Almighty is with us" **(vv. 7, 11)**.

Let us look at each of these sections to see what we can learn about living trustfully in a threatening world.

A. Confidence in the Midst of Commotion (vv. 1–3)

The word *therefore* **(v. 2)** suggests the source of confidence, resulting in diminished fear. The psalmist declares the nearness of his God, who is able to help. God is like a fortress that no enemy can enter. Enemies may surround it, but God is strong and able to defend. The enemies cannot overcome. No wonder Luther sang "A Mighty Fortress Is Our God" when enemies sought to destroy him and thwart his proclamation of the Gospel—salvation by grace *alone* through faith *alone* in Christ *alone*. Let us apply this picture to our world today. Although we are surrounded by commotion, God is near. When we speak with Him, our fear lessens.

1. We are not sure how the psalmist meant us to understand the pictures of shaking mountains and roaring waters, but he sums them all up as *trouble*. There are many possible ways these verses

can speak to us. For example:

    a. Commotion in the earth: earthquakes, hurricanes, floods, famine

    b. Commotion among nations: international strife, rumors of war, war

    c. Commotion in humans: doubts, despair, frustrations, hostilities

    d. Commotion in the church: conflicting doctrines, martyrdom

2. In all these calamities humans seem so small and insignificant, so helpless. But every day God is able to strengthen, keep, and guide through the means of grace—Word and Sacrament.

B. God's Glad City (vv. 4–7)

A second source of release from fear is found in the picture of God's glad city, where the people of God live, surrounded by commotion in the world—*in* the world but not *of* the world. The believers have the comfort that God is always with them. They are also a comfort to each other as they remind each other that God is exalted and able to save.

A *city* is a habitation of many people. In a city we find life together—fellowship. Streets symbolize communication and an interchange of thoughts and feelings.

The city is *glad* because the people are secure in God's presence.

1. The *river* flowing through the city is the presence of God. (See also **Rev. 22:1–5.**) His presence is individualized and comes to each of us in His *streams*—the Word and the sacraments. Through these means God assures us individually of His mercy and love.

2. God promises that His *city* will not fall. (See also **Matt. 16:18.**) The gates of hell shall not prevail against the church. God will give you the strength to "let nothing move you" **(1 Cor. 15:58).**

3. Once again from the ramparts of the glad city, the psalmist sees the nations in uproar. Nowhere in the Bible are we told that God's people will not meet trouble, suffering, or even violent death. Jesus Himself, in His farewell message to the disciples, said, "In this world you will have trouble. But take heart! I have overcome the world" **(John 16:33).** Not *from* troubles but *during* trouble does He keep His own.

When we list all the nations that have fallen during our life span, we are amazed how many there are. Also think of all the countries where Christians have been oppressed, tortured, brainwashed, or killed during our lifetime. Did God fail these persons? Was He not their refuge and strength? From the lips and writings of such martyrs comes the testimony that, when alone with their sufferings, they were yet not alone! Christ comforted them with a great sense of His nearness and flooded them with peace. God helped some with a freedom to forgive and pray for their tormentors. They were God's remnant in the "glad" city, watched over by Him and finally taken home by Him. God's Word and the response in prayer made the difference to these people.

God's power comes through His voice, His Word. God speaks in many ways. Often when we are in the midst of a calamity we do not hear God utter His voice. We read the news items and do not recognize that God has spoken. A newspaper announces the overthrow or death of a dictator; a preacher of repentance warns of judgment upon a nation persisting in sin, and we are unaware that God has spoken. (See **2 Kings 19:32–35; Jonah 3:4–5.**)

"The earth melts"—This is a very human picture of the reaction to judgment. Human courage melts away **(Ps. 107:26; Joshua 2:11).** The earth will melt in the final judgment **(2 Peter 3:12).**

4. **Verses 7** and **11** are identical refrains. The repetition is for emphasis, for reassurance. Two titles are given to God, who is the city's refuge:

a. "The Lord Almighty." This has also been translated as "the Lord of hosts." (See **1 Sam. 17:45; Is. 40:26;** and **Luke 2:13** to identify the hosts.)

b. "The God of Jacob." Although He is the God of nations, He is also the God of one as weak and sinful as Jacob. Jacob represents God's people. God cares for us no matter how weak we are. Let us thank Him for this assurance.

C. Invitation to See God at Work (vv. 8–11)

1. We are invited to view a scene of terrible devastation. It is not modern tanks and missiles that are mentioned, but weapons of the psalmist's day: bow, spear, shield (or chariot). But war is war, and it brings desolation to the earth. We are surprised to read that it is God who has brought the desolation on the earth. Isn't it people who, having hated long enough, resort to killing their enemy? Surely it can't be God's will! No, God's will is that all His children love and help each other. But if, in their estrangement from God, they persist in hating and coveting, God doesn't hold them back from destroying each other. God can use the suffering they have inflicted upon themselves to bring them back to Himself in their helplessness.

2. Until now the psalmist has spoken, but now God says, "Be still." He knows the value of quietness as a remedy for a disturbed people. He also knows the value of quietness, both of silence and not being active, for the individual child of God who gets so frustrated and so busy that he or she doesn't take time to look up to God but only looks down at his or her own problems. Taking time to be still before God, we can recognize Him as the great "I am," who is exalted, who knows how to deal with individuals and nations.

3. We can bravely pass through this world, knowing that God is always

in charge. In **verse 1** the psalmist trusts God and with confidence prays, "God is our refuge and strength, an ever-present help in trouble." In the repeated refrain **(vv. 7** and **11),** he affirms his trust in the Lord of hosts, who is in our midst, and the God of Jacob, who is our refuge.

Conclusion

Close with prayer. You might ask volunteers to pray sentence prayers. Or use a familiar hymn to close.

Lesson 3

God Speaks about the Suffering Messiah (Psalm 22)

Aims

To see the struggle and victory of the psalmist.
To see how Christ fulfilled this psalm on the cross.
To look to Christ in hours of darkness.

Leader's Personal Preparation

1. Ask God to enlighten you with His Holy Spirit.

2. Do the lesson in the Study Guide before class time to familiarize yourself with it.

3. Look at the aims and keep them in mind during the study.

4. After studying the psalm, summarize what this psalm has said to you.

Introduction to the Lesson

Begin with devotions. An appropriate Scripture passage to read is **Matt. 27:45–46.**

Set the mood of the study with a short reminder of the meaning of the season of Lent. You may want to have some Lenten books available. Call the members' attention to them. Encourage the group to talk a bit about what Lent means to them.

Studying the Psalm

I. The Story of the Psalm

This study has two main themes: (1) the psalm in relation to David's life, and (2) its fulfillment in the life of Christ. Go quickly over the first part in order to be able to spend a great deal of time on the messianic element in the psalm.

A. David's Cry of Anguish (vv. 1–21)

After David wonders why God does not answer and help him, he reminds God that his fathers trusted in Him and were saved. But then David does some self-evaluating and admits that he is only a worm—scorned, despised, and mocked by the people. Again he speaks to God, who has been with him since birth and whom he needs now, because he is encompassed by vicious people. David's mood goes *down, down, down* as he is laid low physically. Once more he pleads for help and deliverance as he again sees how he is surrounded by evildoers.

B. David's Song of Praise (vv. 22–31)

Suddenly his mood changes. Now David bursts forth with a song of thanks and praise. His mood goes *up, up, up* and his cry of triumph ends with the words "He has done it." He anticipates what God will do for him.

Beginning with his own declaration of praise, he invites an ever-widening circle of people and nations to join him. He begins with "I will declare"; then he invites, "You who fear the Lord, praise Him!" Then the invitation goes to the great assembly, all the afflicted who seek God, all the ends of the earth, all families of the nations, the rich, posterity, and the unborn coming generations. All are to join in a doxology of praise to God.

II. Christ and This Psalm

A. While this psalm is the experience of David, who cried out in despair, "My God, my God, why have You forsaken me?" it is also the experience that belongs to all believers and has been felt by saintly sufferers in all ages. Yet the voice that rang through the darkness on Calvary was the cry of Christ, who experienced death's force in supreme measure and in a unique manner. Only He knew the mortal agony of utter separation from God. Only He clung to God in absolute trust, even in the darkest moments. That which separated Him was the gathered sins of the whole world laid on Him and accepted by Him in the perfection of His loving identification of Himself with all people.

Verse 15 describes the thirst of Christ upon the hill of Golgotha. Of this John writes, "Later, knowing that all was now completed, and so that the Scripture would be fulfilled, Jesus said, 'I am thirsty'" **(John 19:28).**

Verses 16–18 picture very vividly the scene of the crucifixion. A company of evildoers and mockers surrounded Jesus. They pierced His hands and His feet when He was placed upon the cross. One writer says of **verse 17,** "The picture of bodily sufferings has one more touch in 'I can count all my bones.'" Emaciation would produce that effect, but so would crucifixion, which extended the frame and threw the bones of the thorax into prominence. Then the sufferer turns his eyes once more to his enemies and describes the gloating with which they fed upon his agonies. Crucifixion was a slow process, and we recall the long hours in which the crowd satisfied its hatred through its eyes. The soldiers divided the garments of Christ and cast lots for His robe.

B. Although the second half of this psalm describes David's song of praise, it amazingly anticipates the Gospel of Christ's redemption being told throughout the world. It previews the power of this Gospel and the lordship of Christ, at whose feet all nations will bow. The rich and the poor worship Him. People will tell of the Lord even to generations yet unborn. Christ fulfilled these Scriptures centuries later. These Old Testament pictures greatly enrich our understanding of our Messiah and His redemptive work.

III. Parallel Experiences of David and Jesus

There are some details in the affliction of David that were quite similar to those of Christ. Of David it is told that he fled crying, found no rest, and was despised by his own people. **2 Samuel 15** tells of David's people rejecting him in favor of Absalom and how because of this he fled for his life. In **verses 23** and **30** we read that David wept as he passed over the brook Kidron and went up the Mount of Olives, despised and rejected. Jesus later retraced these steps. **Isaiah 53** gives us the picture of God's servant rejected, a man of sorrows.

IV. David's Enemies Compared to Wild Animals (vv. 12, 13, 16, 20, 21)

In **verse 12** we read of the bulls of Bashan. Bashan was famous for its rich pastureland. Bulls of this area were known for their strength. David uses this term to suggest the strength and rage of his enemies. He also compares them to roaring lions (**vv. 13, 21**). Packs of wild, savage dogs haunted Eastern villages. They reminded David of his enemies—fierce, contemptible men. In Jesus' day the word *dog* was used to express contempt for Gentiles. In the story of the Canaanite woman, Jesus quotes this word but softens it with a word not meaning "dog" but "doggie," a loved pet. (See **Matt. 15:26–27.**) Wild oxen also are mentioned by David to describe the cruelty of his enemies.

V. David's Physical and Emotional Suffering (vv. 14–15)

Knowing that his own son and his own people were plotting his death nearly broke David's heart. With this grief went the anguish that his son might smite the capital city, which David loved, with the edge of the sword (see **2 Sam. 15:14**). Going in haste and fleeing from his murderous son must have exhausted David physically. The Hebrew way of describing physical or emotional breakdown is to speak of broken bones. We might say, "My bones ached"; "I nearly went to pieces"; "I was all in." David said he was poured out like water. We might say, "This took all the starch out of me." In other words, we do not take the words literally, but as the description of a feeling. To be sure, the parching effect of fear and fever causes the tongue to be dry.

VI. How Help Came (v. 21)

What happened to lift David's pitiful prayer into a glorious song of praise is indicated in a footnote to **verse 21** (in some translations), which reads "You have heard." What a change comes to a human heart when the person is assured that God has not forgotten or ignored him or her, but has heard! This was Christ's experience, too, on the cross. After saying, "My God, why?" He was able to once again call God "Father," knowing that He had been heard in heaven.

The words of **verse 22** are repeated by Christ in **Heb. 2:12.**

VII. The Poor Will Eat (v. 26)

In the Old Testament days if someone wanted to thank God for a special blessing, he or she brought a thankoffering of food, part of which could be eaten on the day it was offered (see **Leviticus 7**). The reference to such eating in **verse 26** could apply either to the offering brought by a thankful person or to the offering presented by David, in which others were invited to share.

VIII. "He Has Done It" (v. 31)

With these words of victory the psalm ends. In fulfillment Christ said, "It is finished"—our salvation is a done deal. We celebrate our eternal victory!

Conclusion

Close the meeting with prayer, either by several individuals or by one person praying for the group.

Lesson 4

God Speaks about Forgiveness
(Psalm 32)

Aims

To learn what to do with sin and guilt.

To see the consequences of neglected guilt.

To rejoice in God's abundant forgiveness through Christ.

Leader's Personal Preparation

1. Do the lesson in the Study Guide before class time to familiarize yourself with it. Think of the members of your study group as you prepare, breathing a prayer that each of them will be helped through the group study.

2. Carefully read the introduction and Bible study helps for this lesson in this guide. Make notes for yourself as you read.

3. When you have finished your study of the psalm, tell yourself in one or two sentences what God has said to you personally.

Introduction to the Lesson

1. Your attitude of anticipation of something wonderful will be contagious. Be sure you are well prepared and eager to lead.

2. Begin your discussion by reading the psalm together or having it read. You might have it read in more than one translation if they are available. Draw attention to the divisions and headings of the sections as you do this reading. The psalm divides into two basic sections: **verses 1–5,** where the psalmist speaks of his personal experience. In light of this he goes on to exhort others in **verses 6–11.** Note the conjunction *therefore,* which ties the two sections together. Observe also the following divisions, which are denoted by the titles in the Bible Study Helps section:

Forgiveness brings blessedness (**vv. 1–2**)

The consequences of unconfessed sin (**vv. 3–4**)

Confession brings forgiveness (**v. 5**)

Exhortation (**vv. 6–9**)

Rejoice (**vv. 10–11**)

3. Following the reading of the psalm, proceed through the Bible study, taking time for individuals to share whatever understanding they receive. Encourage those who have done some of the additional study under "More Understanding" to share their enrichment. The heart of this lesson is to

struggle with the seriousness of unconfessed sin and guilt, to understand God's great grace in the forgiveness of sins through Christ, and to receive and be assured of this forgiveness.

Studying the Psalm

A. Forgiveness Brings Blessedness (vv. 1–2)

The word *blessed* is properly translated "Oh, how happy" or "how fortunate." Thus David says to us, "Oh, how happy, how fortunate is he who has heard the good news of forgiveness; who, in a personal experience, has accepted this forgiveness. He can shout for joy."

For emphasis David uses various words to describe our disobedience to God. They all mean practically the same thing. The word *transgression* suggests going beyond or violating the Law of God (such as the Ten Commandments). Actually the Hebrew word is much stronger, emphasizing the element of rebellion or the clash of wills. The word *sin* covers any thought, word, action, omission, or desire contrary to the moral law of God; failure to hit the mark of perfection. The word *iniquity* refers to perversity or crookedness of any kind, as well as the guilt of the evildoer.

B. The Consequences of Unconfessed Sin (vv. 3–4)

It is believed that David, the friend of God, refused to admit and confess his sin for a long time. He describes that time as a time when God's hand was heavy upon him. He felt choked, but he still loved his sin (which was the taking of another man's wife, **2 Samuel 11–12**).

Estrangement from God results from neglecting our guilt. Have you ever experienced that when you were plagued by the memory of some unworthy thing in your life it was hard to talk to God? The longer you were stubborn or careless or frightened about this matter, the farther away God seemed to you. Not until you finally cast yourself upon His merciful forgiveness were you ready to listen to Him speak through the Word, or to be comfortable in prayer.

Guilt brings undue tension. Whether we are willing to do something about it or not, the tension guilt causes may bring physical breakdown. A person in guilt is waging an inner civil war, admitting, denying, excusing, polishing up sin, denying the consequences thereof, and hating self for it. Disgust and shame end in fear. These feelings bring tension, which in turn may bring emotionally induced illnesses. Doctors today recognize that such maladies as headaches, loss of appetite, sleeplessness, or even some cases of arthritis, ulcers, or eczema may be caused or aggravated by tension produced by guilt. David describes his feeling of illness with the words "My bones wasted away . . . my strength was sapped." He may also have lost appetite and strength, or perhaps even developed an ulcer.

C. Confession Brings Forgiveness (v. 5)

At last David said to himself, "How stupid I am! There is forgiveness. Yes, I am a sinner—God, forgive me!"

David's testimony, "And You forgave the guilt of my sin," reminds us of Jesus' promise in **John 6:37,** "Whoever comes to Me I will never drive away." There is no need of coaxing an unwilling God. One honest, contrite, humble cry to God for mercy reaches His ear and He acts. The joy that accompanies the final release from guilt is proof of its reality. (Read **Is. 57:15.**)

But some say, "I did confess my sin and found no peace. In fact, I have honestly confessed it dozens of times. Am I not sorry enough, or what is wrong?"

There are two answers that may help if you are feeling this way: (1) Assurance that you are forgiven does not depend on your feelings, but on God's promises and faithfulness. Therefore, if you have confessed your sin and claimed forgiveness, quiet your heart by repeating as often as you need the assurance "If we confess our sins, He is faithful and just and will forgive us our sins and purify us from all unrighteousness" **(1 John 1:9).** Then thank the Lord over and over that it is a fact you are forgiven and you need not go by your feelings. *Then act as if you are forgiven.* David did! (See **Ps. 130:4.**)

(2) If after that you still have no peace, talk out your guilt feelings with a Christian friend, pastor, or counselor. Listen to Jesus: "Again, I tell you that if two of you on earth agree about anything you ask for, it will be done for you by My Father in heaven. For where two or three come together in My name, there am I with them" **(Matt. 18:19–20).** Some people who are bowed down by an abnormal, haunting guilt may need psychiatric help. David's experience was similar to that which most of us have most of the time, when we find release and peace as soon as we come to the Lord for forgiveness, unworthy though we be. Someone has said, "The Christian church is the only society in the world that is based on the single qualification that the candidate is unworthy of membership."

D. Exhortation (vv. 6–9)

1. David commends the practice of prayer. He wishes everyone would take his experience as an example.

2. David again expresses his own confidence in God. Notice that he speaks in the present tense in **verse 7**—not "Once You were my hiding place," but always "You *are.*"

3. In these verses it is not clear whether David is speaking the instructions of God or whether God Himself is speaking. Whichever interpretation

is used, the exhortation comes from God. He promises to do three wonderful things: to instruct, to teach, and to counsel. He even tells us how He will do these—namely, by watching over us. Read **Ps. 34:15–16** and note that the eyes of the Lord can be *upon* or *against* us, depending on whether we are "righteous" or whether we "do evil." Notice how Peter quotes this thought in his first epistle **(1 Peter 3:12)**.

God is watching over us! Is this a comforting thought or an uncomfortable one? In **Psalm 139** David thinks it is wonderful and prays in **verses 23–24,** "Search me, O God, and know my heart; test me and know my anxious thoughts. See if there is any offensive way in me, and lead me in the way everlasting."

4. If we understand God's instruction and guidance, we ought not be like dumb animals such as a horse or mule, who must be controlled by a bit and bridle. God will lead us where He wants us to go and will keep us with Him.

E. Rejoice (vv. 10–11)

The concluding verses contrast miserable people, who harbor unconfessed sin, and the righteous, who know the experience of forgiveness and know the joy it brings. These verses tell us that righteous people are surrounded by the unfailing love of God. They are upright in heart with a renewed motivation and purpose for life. They trust in the Lord and have reason to rejoice and shout for joy in their new state of grace.

Conclusion

Close the lesson with prayers of thanksgiving for God's great love, or with a prayer asking Him for forgiveness.

Lesson 5

God Speaks When I Am Moody
(Psalms 42 and 43)

Aims

To see the cause for moods and affirm its cure.

Leader's Personal Preparation

1. Take time to read the "Instructions for the Leader" at the beginning of

this guide. Read again how you are to be the encourager, the enabler, and the intercessor. Remember that you are not to lecture or to give all the answers. You are to guide the meeting by enlisting the members to share what they have discovered.

2. You will need the help of the Holy Spirit. Invite Him in prayer to open your eyes to behold wondrous things in these psalms.

3. Carefully do the lesson in the Study Guide before class time. Read the introduction and Bible study helps in this guide. It is important that you be well-prepared. Only then can you do a good job of leading.

4. Notice the aim for this study. When you have conducted the study, you will want to look at the aim again and see if it has been accomplished.

Introduction to the Lesson

The opening devotions should lead into the spirit of the lesson. You might have the group read **Psalm 130.**

As a group, read **Psalms 42** and **43,** with one person reading the refrain in **verses 42:5, 11,** and **43:5.** Then break into smaller units and assign parts of the discussion section to each group. Ask each group to reread the section of the psalm to which their questions relate. Allow at least 10 minutes for the groups to grapple with the questions. At the end of the time, go through the discussion questions, asking each group to report on its findings. Invite others to contribute their ideas as well. Encourage those who have done outside reading and enrichment study to share what they have learned as you proceed through their study. Take plenty of time to relate the struggles of the psalmist to the struggles of Christian living today. Let the participants share the moods that they have experienced and how they have found restored hope and joy.

Studying the Psalms

As you read the inscription, note that **Psalm 42** is a *maskil,* which may mean that it is a psalm of instruction. Note, too, that it is attributed to the sons of Korah. These men are believed to have been a guild of Levites who compiled collections of psalms.

Psalms 42 and **43** are studied together for several reasons:

1. They are closely connected by similarity of style and content.

2. **Psalm 43** is an "orphan," having no separate title.

3. Both psalms belong to a time when worship in the temple was in full activity.

The writer of both psalms may have been a Levite who was detained in the north of Palestine and beset by heathen enemies who taunted him about his God.

Note how the refrains divide the psalms into three parts, with the psalmist telling how he feels in each:

1. When he is excluded from the temple service where he wanted to be with fellow worshipers, and also when he is mocked for his longing for God **(42:1–5)**

2. When he finds that he is miles away from where he longed to be, and he feels forgotten by God—and for this, too, his enemies mock him by saying, "Where is your God?" **(42:6–10)**

3. When he must live and deal with difficult people **(43)**.

Let us look at each of these situations and see what we can learn for ourselves.

A. The Psalmist Longs for God (42:1–5)

In the garden of Eden God came to walk and talk with Adam and Eve. They ran to meet Him. He spoke to them. When sin broke this perfect relationship, the first humans took their unsatisfied longing for God with them out of the garden into a cold world. All through the ages and in every tribe and nation the longing for God can be traced. That is what we have, you and I. It is within us, a heart crying out for peace with God. Job cried, "If only I knew where to find Him; if only I could go to His dwelling!" **(Job 23:3)**. God answered such plaintive cries, "You will seek Me and find Me when you seek Me with all your heart" **(Jer. 29:13)**. Paul, preaching on Mars Hill **(Acts 17,** emphasis added), said, "From one man He made every nation of men . . . *that men would seek Him* and perhaps reach out for Him and find Him, though He is not far from each one of us." God wants to answer the longing of our hearts.

As we study human history, we see that all through the ages people have made for themselves something to worship. The heathen used wood and stone to make a god to satisfy their longing to worship. Native Americans, not knowing the true God, longed for the Great Spirit and his happy hunting ground. The Athenians made altars to many gods. The origin of the word *religion* is "to bind fast," people seeking to bind or tie themselves to the god they believe has made them. But how about us today? It almost seems as if we are an exception. We seem to have lost that longing. We seem to get along fine without God. And yet if we look deeper, we find that the longing is there although unrecognized. There is a little feeling of never being satisfied, always wanting something more. If we get money, we want more. If we have one car, we think we "need" a second one. Somewhere we must find something that will satisfy! Are we church members guilty of the same thing, seeking satisfaction in things? Or do we long for God and seek Him with our whole heart and, finding Him, live contentedly and thankfully?

When life gets hard, people become moody. To learn what is really meant by the word *mood*, we go to Webster. He says a mood is a particular state of mind or feeling. Thus we may be in a sullen mood and display ill humor or be unsociable, sulky, or glum. Or we may be in a happy state of mind and display good will, gladness, lightness, and fun. Moods can vary all the way from hilarity to despair. Our vocabulary today is full of such words as *frustrated, insecure, depressed, irritated, blue, let-down, restless, worried, discouraged, sad,* and *mad.* What can the cause be? What is the cure?

Ps. 42:1–5 shows us an example of *frustration* because of a spoiled plan, and frustration because people could not understand an inner need. The psalmist longed for the temple services. In **verses 1–2** the psalmist lets us look into his troubled heart, filled with longing and thirst for God. He is not ashamed to admit that he has wept over his situation. He wonders when he will ever get back to Jerusalem to behold God's face in a temple experience.

Two further matters increase his suffering: (1) Persons whom he describes in **43:1** as "ungodly" make fun of his God, asking, "Where is your God?" We are reminded of Christ's experience on the cross. (Read **Luke 23:35–37.**) (2) Unbearable longing fills him as he remembers the wonderful processions up to the temple, the multitudes singing as they went. **Psalms 120** to **134** are all titled as songs of ascents. These may have been the psalms the processions sang as they ascended the mount to the temple. A similar longing is expressed in **Psalm 137** by the Israelites as they are in Babylonian bondage.

Do we not have the same frustrations? We plan and save for a home, but the plan is spoiled by sickness and huge doctor bills. We plan all year for a vacation trip only to find when the time comes that there is a transportation strike and we cannot go. We desire to have a real Christian home, but some member of the family objects to family devotions, to table prayer, to church attendance. The person cannot see our longing for God and for family solidarity through prayer and praise. There is tension. We don't want to give up our hopes and ideals. Situations and people won't cooperate. We can't force our way through. We are tense. We are frustrated.

How does release come? The psalmist followed this course: (1) He shed tears; he grieved as he looked at his problem in all its complexity. (2) He asked himself, "Why do I feel so deeply about this? Why am I so disturbed, so worried? Why do I let this color my whole life?" (3) He encouraged himself to hope in God. After all, God was still there. (4) He felt better already and became confident. "I will yet praise Him." (5) His personal relationship to God was repaired so that he could say, "My Savior and my God."

Such release is available to us. Let us do as the psalmist did: (1) Let us admit to ourselves that sometimes we can't change the situation, sad as it may be. Let us admit that in ourselves we can do little but grieve, shed tears, be frustrated, or be angry.

(2) Let us ask ourselves as the psalmist did, "Is it really worth going to pieces over? Do I want to become a problem to myself and my family because I can't have my way, right as it may be? Is there nothing I can be happy about and thankful for? Does no one understand? Must I carry the load alone?"

(3) We need to tell ourselves as the psalmist did, "Hope in God." We need to remind ourselves that God is still there. He can bring good out of each situation. He can guide us in what to do next. He can make us wise to know how to act. He can lead us step by step. He can help us to be strong and courageous and to "take it." Then let's unburden the whole load on Him, for He said, "Come to Me, all you who are weary and burdened, and I will give you rest" **(Matt. 11:28)**.

(4) And immediately we need to *act as if* God has our situation in His hand. We need to see ourselves changed from a frustrated being to a courageous, calm one. Although we cannot see *how* God will help, we need to act as if He is already at work. Then praise will come over our lips. (5) Our testimony now will be "my Savior and my God." We will have something to tell others about God's nearness and love.

B. The Psalmist Feels Forgotten by God (42:6–11)

In these verses we see an example of depression. The psalmist finds himself miles away from where he longs desperately to be, and he feels forgotten by God while his enemies mock, "Where is your God?"

The psalmist finds himself in the north of Palestine, where the Jordan has its origin, far away from Jerusalem. The exact location of Mount Mizar is not known. The word *Mizar* means "little." Therefore, the mount may have been too little to be on the map. Look for Mount Hermon on your map. In this distant place the psalmist feels forgotten by God. The aloneness of a soul, the forsakenness by God, is unbearable to humans. Even Christ on the cross cried out in anguish when He felt forsaken.

Using word pictures, the psalmist tried to help us feel as he did. The first picture he gives is that of a cascade rushing down from Mount Hermon when the snow melts in the spring. One waterfall plunges to another; one trouble comes on top of another. Waves and breakers probably describe the flooding of a river. Disquieting thoughts and waves of longing for the temple, but most of all the feelings of forsakenness, flood his soul.

Yet even in the midst of all this, God grants him His steadfast love and makes possible a song and a prayer, so that the psalmist is able to call God "my Rock." This is yet another word picture. A rock, dashed by breakers and waves, is standing secure as the Rock of Ages, which floods cannot wash away. His enemies continue to taunt him.

Do we not have similar trials and moods? We, too, may find ourselves miles away from dear ones whose nearness means much to us. We may be lonely, homesick, depressed. We may find ourselves unable to attend an event, a special occasion that would mean so very much to us, and we are glum. We remember the "good old days," but it is all so different now, and we are irritated. We remember when our family was intact, and we were all so happy. Now a dear one is missing, and we are lonely and sad. We remember Christmas and how precious God seemed to us as we sang of Christ the Savior being born. Now we dread the coming of Christmas and are cheerless. We remember how active we were in the work of the church and how we loved the Lord. Now we sit helpless in a wheelchair in a nursing home, lonely and depressed. Trouble over trouble, like a waterfall plunging from one depth to another, piles up. One mood of depression follows another until we finally cannot pray anymore, and we ask, "Has God forgotten me?"

How did release come? The psalmist followed this course of action: (1) During the day and also at night he kept praying. (2) His prayer was a song containing thoughts of God's steadfast love, of God as his Rock. He told God that he felt forgotten, and he demanded to know why God would forget him and why he has to go mourning because of his enemies. (3) He repeated his previous conversation with himself, asking the same question and affirming the same hope.

Such release is available to us. Prayer is our greatest help when struggling with a heavy heart. We dare to do as the psalmist did and tell God just how we feel. We can even use the psalmist's words to express our feelings if we can't express our depression in our own words. We read that Jesus, when He was in Gethsemane, began to be sorrowful and troubled. He said, "My soul is overwhelmed with sorrow to the point of death" **(Mark 14:34)**. Jesus admitted to the Father how He felt. We can too. Jesus was sorrowful and troubled. We often are too. Jesus came out of His heaviness triumphant, not because the plan of suffering was changed, but because He could go through with it. He could say, "Yet not what I will, but what You will" **(Mark 14:36)**. We, too, shall be able to say and even sing, "Have Thine own way, Lord." Way back in the 17th century Georg Neumark penned a wonderful hymn in which he testified to God's faithfulness, if we but come to Him with our depressions:

If you but trust in God to guide you
And place your confidence in Him,
You'll find Him always there beside you
To give you hope and strength within.
For those who trust God's changeless love
Build on the rock that will not move.

What gain is there in futile weeping,
In helpless anger and distress?
If you are in His care and keeping,
In sorrow will He love you less?
For He who took for you a cross
Will bring you safe through ev'ry loss.

In patient trust await His leisure
In cheerful hope, with heart content
To take whate'er your Father's pleasure
And all-discerning love have sent;
Doubt not your inmost wants are known
To Him who chose you for His own.

Sing, pray, and keep His ways unswerving,
Offer your service faithfully,
And trust His word; though undeserving,
You'll find His promise true to be.
God never will forsake in need
The soul that trusts in Him indeed.

Text from *Lutheran Book of Worship*, copyright © 1978. By permission of Concordia Publishing House.

C. The Psalmist Prays for Restored Joy (43)

In **Psalm 43** we see an example of irritation, when the psalmist had to deal with difficult people. People are his trouble now. The psalmist mentions three sorts: the ungodly, the deceitful, and the wicked. He prays God to vindicate him, to defend him, and to rescue him.

To stop his irritation and his mourning, he asks for two helps. Knowing that he can't change his enemies, he asks for (1) light from God on how to act and feel, and (2) truth to lead him, truth that God has not forgotten him. With these, like two angels, one at either side, he knows he shall be led back to Jerusalem, back to the temple, back to the altar of God, there to praise his God with a harp. (This was a stringed instrument, much smaller and with fewer strings than the harps of today.) There he will say, "O God, *my* God."

How irritating for us, too, to have an ungodly spouse, child, in-law, employer, employee, or neighbor who taunts us about our faith in God. The tension finally becomes unbearable and oppressive, and we become sick of it all. How irritating for us, too, to have an unjust and deceitful landlord, business firm, co-worker—anyone!

How did release come? The psalmist followed this course: (1) He asked God to vindicate him against ungodly people. To vindicate means to clear from accusation of guilt; to defend; to prove right. The adversaries taunted him that he was stupid enough to believe in God. The psalmist, therefore, asks God to show them that He is in control and that they are wrong. (2) He asked God to deliver him from deceitful and unjust men—an honest plea for help. (3) With mixed emotions he tells God he is taking refuge in Him, but still he wonders why God has cast him off and lets him be oppressed by his enemies. (4) What he needs are two great helps from God: God's light and God's truth to release him from his irritation. For these he asks. (5) But once more he chides himself that at the same time that he asks God for victory, he is still cast down.

Such release is available to us also. Let us do as the psalmist did. (1) We, too, can ask God to vindicate us when people make fun of our faith and our church-going. An older single woman who had worked hard for many years in a factory gave liberally and cheerfully to the work of God's kingdom. Her ungodly relatives always jeered at her for her generosity, saying, "You just shovel your hard-earned money out, and what do you get for it!" She finally defended her cause by replying with a twinkle in her eye, "All right, I may shovel it out, but God eventually shovels it back in blessings, and His shovel is bigger than mine!" (2) The psalmist, knowing he couldn't change people, asked God to do with them what is right. This is exactly what Peter told us to do. "But how is it to your credit if you receive a beating for doing wrong and endure it? But if you suffer for doing good and you endure it, this is commendable before God. To this you were called, because Christ suffered for you, leaving you an example, that you should follow in His steps. . . . When they hurled their insults at Him, He did not retaliate; when He suffered, He made no threats. Instead He entrusted Himself to Him who judges justly" **(1 Peter 2:20–23).** (3) We, too, need to ask for light on the situation, light on how to behave, what to do and what not to do. Also we need to be filled with God's truth—that He loves us, that He knows about our irritation, that He cares. Step by step He will guide us and relieve our trouble, or give us good cheer if it is not removed. We therefore dare to wait without irritation, putting our hope in Him to work things out. Remember **Is. 40:31,** "Those who hope in the Lord will renew their strength."

Conclusion

At the end of the period it would be well if you as the leader could summarize some of the main teachings of this lesson. The Bible study helps in this guide should be helpful.

Close the meeting with prayer. Try to vary prayer experiences from time to time. You may ask for individual prayers or silent prayer, read a prayer from the hymnal or some other source, ask an individual to pray for the group, or lead in a closing prayer yourself.

When you get home, take a few moments to think through how the meeting went, where it was strong, where it was weak, and what you hope to avoid the next time. If ever a study does not go well, do not get discouraged. Talk it over with God and anticipate a better meeting next time if you are the leader again.

Lesson 6

God Speaks about the Great Creator
(Psalm 104)

Aims

To become more aware of beauty around us.

To think of God when we see beauty.

To demonstrate joy as our thoughts linger on the beauty of God's creation and His love for us in Christ.

Leader's Personal Preparation

1. Do the lesson in the Study Guide before class time. Read the introduction and Bible study helps in this guide.

2. Pray for the guidance of the Holy Spirit as you do your studying. Pray for each member of your study group and for God's presence with your group as you meet together.

3. Look around for pictures of nature. Mount them for display at the group meeting. Or you may ask someone who has some slides of nature scenes to bring a few to the meeting for the group to enjoy. The psalm could be read as the group looks at a series of beautiful slides.

4. **Psalm 104** is a poem of praise for the wonders of God's creation. Bring to your place of study some objects of nature that fill you with awe

and wonder, such as a rose, a tiny buttercup from among the grasses, even a dandelion, a weed with lacy seed pods, a pine cone, a feather, a stone, a shell, or anything else of which you can say, "Look, isn't this pretty!" Look at every detail. You may note the shades of color, shapes, and fragrances. Then bow your head and thank God.

If you are doing your lesson at night, go to the window—or better yet, go outdoors—and look up at the stars and the moon. Look at them for a long time. Perhaps you have a nature book on stars. Page through it and marvel at the groupings. Do the same with a bird book. Look for color in everything about you in the room. Then thank God. If you have a pet—a bird, a cat, a dog—study and admire it and thank God that He even thought of our pleasure when He made pets for us.

5. If you have time, read a few nature poems. You may want to share one with your group.

6. Now you are ready to read **Psalm 104** and to make detailed observations. Stop at each wonder of creation the poet mentions and thank God for it.

Introduction to the Lesson

Begin with devotions. Today's devotions might emphasize our thankfulness for God's creation. Read a nature poem or show pictures, slides, or some object of nature. Ask volunteers to give thanks to God for items of His creation in one-sentence prayers (God, I thank You for . . .).

Read **Psalm 104** as the basis for discussion. You might divide the class into three groups, having each group read one of the parts of the psalm. This reading may precede the entire discussion, and each part of the psalm may be reread just before it is discussed.

While this psalm mentions many things in creation, the emphasis is really on the Creator and His greatness. In looking at the marvels of God's creation all around us, we may be tempted to think only of the beauty of nature and fail to see in it the God who has made and who sustains all things. As we observe God's wonderful creation, we also must notice the disharmony that people and their sinfulness and disobedience have brought into the picture. Share this concept with the group and call their attention to **verse 35,** where the psalmist prays that God would remove this disharmony.

Studying the Psalm

During his ministry, Paul wrote to the Christians at Philippi, "Whatever is lovely . . . think about such things" **(Phil. 4:8).** Nature gives us so much that is lovely to think about.

Remember that this psalm is poetry and not a textbook on natural science. Details of these word pictures are not to be studied scientifically. They simply express the glory of God's activity.

This is one of four hymns of the Psalter that center in praise to God as the great Creator (**Psalm 8; 19:1–6; 29;** and **104**). The creation account in **Genesis 1** can be studied in relation to this psalm.

A. The Heavens (vv. 1–4)

The psalmist summons himself to bless God for His greatness, honor, and majesty. Although this psalm is an "orphan," without an indication of authorship, it is believed that the same author wrote both **Psalm 103** and **104**. Note how both psalms begin and end.

Verses 1–4 center around the heavens.

1. *Light* is God's garment. (See **Gen. 1:3** and note that calling light into being was the first activity of creation.)

2. God stretches out the heavens as easily as a person stretches out a tent curtain. (See **Amos 9:6.**) He rides in the clouds and the wind. To better understand **verses 3** and **4**, read **Gen. 1:6–7** and **Amos 9:6.**

B. The Earth (vv. 5–9)

This account parallels that in **Gen. 1:9; 7:17–20;** and **9:11–15.** The one true God speaks, and the waters covering the earth recede to their appointed bounds. God's command to the waters is described as having been uttered in thunder.

C. The Water (vv. 10–13)

By springs and rain God provides the necessary water for animals, birds, and people. There is no exact parallel for these verses in **Genesis 1**, but rain and streams are mentioned in **Gen. 2:5–6.**

D. The Vegetation (vv. 14–18)

These verses parallel **Gen. 1:11–12.** God provides grass for cattle; food-plants, wine, olive oil, and bread for people; and trees for the birds.

E. Moon and Sun (vv. 19–23)

Compare these verses with **Gen. 1:14–19.**

1. The moon is important because it marks time. When the psalmist wrote this, the moon was very important in marking the times for the religious festivals.

2. Night is mentioned before daylight because the Hebrew day began in the evening. (See **Gen. 1:5, 8, 13, 19, 23, 31.**) Darkness is part of God's good providence so that the wild beasts, including the young lions, may seek their food.

3. God ordained daytime for people to work.

F. The Sea (vv. 24–26)
Verse 24 is a general statement about God's works. (Compare **Ps. 19:1–6; Prov. 3:19; 8:22–31.**) **Verses 25–26** are in part parallel to **Gen. 1:20–21.**
1. Take some time to list some of the animals that live in water.
2. In addition to the innumerable creatures with which the sea teems, the psalmist also thinks of the man-made ships that excite his wonder. Yet even the greatest man-made object pales in comparison to God's creation.
3. In the Old Testament the meaning of the word *leviathan* varies. In **Is. 27:1** it refers to a gliding, coiling serpent. In **Job 41:1** it may refer to a large crocodile. At any rate, it was a huge marine animal, possibly even a whale.

G. Life (vv. 27–30)
1. "These all" refers to all the creatures the psalmist has mentioned, including people.
2. God provides food for all His creation, even to the point where some animals feed on other animals. Scientists call this a "food chain." God made people responsible for overseeing that the balance of nature is not upset.
3. "When You hide Your face" means the withdrawing of God's provision. When God withdraws the breath He gave them, creatures die and return to dust.
4. God sends forth His creative Spirit to renew the earth with new life.

H. Praise to the Creator (vv. 31–35)
1. The psalmist expresses the desire that the glory of God, which is seen in creation, may continue into the indefinite future and that God may find joyous satisfaction in His work. (See **Gen. 1:31.**)
2. He remembers the awesome fact that the Creator can destroy the world He has made. When He looks at the earth, it trembles. When He touches the mountains, they smoke.
3. As God rejoices in His work, so the psalmist rejoices in God and sings praises to Him. **Verse 35** is the psalmist's way of praying that God will remove all the disharmony from His creation. "Praise the Lord" is the Hebrew *Hallelu Yah.*

Conclusion
As a conclusion to the discussion, you might have the group read together **verses 1a** and **35b** of today's psalm.

Lesson 7

God Speaks about National Distress
(Psalms 124 and 67)

Aims

To see where help for a nation is to be found.
To be encouraged to pray more faithfully for our country.

Leader's Personal Preparation

1. Do the lesson in the Study Guide before class time. Read the introduction and Bible study helps in this guide.

2. You may want to line up some patriotic material to take to class, such as flags; maps of your country; a poster of different coins and paper money; pictures of national leaders, past and present; skyline pictures of cities; pictures of rural areas of your country; pictures of roadways.

3. Prayerfully think of all that your country has given to you and what you can give to your country.

4. Study the psalms carefully. Summarize what they say to you.

Introduction to the Lesson

Because these psalms reflect national thanksgiving, begin with a patriotic song, preferably "God Bless Our Native Land." An appropriate prayer would be the prayer of Daniel for his people **(Daniel 9:4–10, 16–19)**. Have the group read the two pledges in the Study Guide. (If you are studying this outside the U.S.A., substitute your country's pledge to the flag or another pledge of citizenship.)

Next, have the group read **Psalms 124** and **67**. Following this, discuss the items you feel are most relevant to your group. It might be better in this instance to discuss fewer of the issues than to try to talk about them all superficially. Stress the importance of Christians taking responsibility in the affairs of our nation seriously.

Studying the Psalms

A. Psalm 124—A Psalm of Gratitude for National Deliverance

This psalm is one of a collection called the songs of ascents. Notice that all the psalms from **120** through **134** are thus named. Bible scholars seem to agree for the most part that these were sung by Jewish pilgrims going up (ascending) on their annual journey to keep the various feasts at Jerusalem. When the procession came within view of Mt. Moriah, on which the temple stood, it broke forth into singing.

These songs, once so well-suited for pilgrims on the way to the temple, are equally well-suited for us Christians today.

National security is a matter of grave concern to our leaders and citizens alike. Who and where are those who threaten our well-being? How can we deal successfully with them? Where is our hope and help? Would that our citizens and leaders would look for the answers in God, where they are to be found. We Christians have the responsibility to vote for and send to our city, state or provincial, and national governments men and women who are willing to listen to God's instructions and seek His guidance.

The Lord, speaking through Solomon **(2 Chron. 7:14),** says, "If My people, who are called by My name, will humble themselves and pray and seek My face and turn from their wicked ways, then will I hear from heaven and will forgive their sin and will heal their land." A good prayer for us Christians is "Lord, give us leaders who will be willing to be led by You."

The Feast of Purim may have been the occasion when this psalm was sung by the Jews to commemorate their deliverance from their enemy, a Persian official called Haman. Esther, the queen, was a beautiful and virtuous woman, loyal to her Jewish people. She risked her life to save her people. Haman had thrown lots to ascertain on which day the bloody massacre of all Jews was to take place. The word *Pur* means "lot"; hence the name *Purim.*

This is a beautiful story of deliverance. The Jews were saved, and Haman, who had plotted the massacre, was destroyed. Be sure to read the story in the book of **Esther.** Point out that just as God used Esther to rescue His people from annihilation, so He rescued us through Jesus Christ from eternal annihilation.

Although the subject of prayer is not mentioned in the story of Esther, it certainly is implied. Let us, therefore, also faithfully intercede for our fellow citizens and leaders that we may face our national and personal enemies in the name of the Lord.

1. This psalm tells us exactly where our help is to be found. After telling us of the danger **(vv. 1–5)** that had threatened the Jewish people, the psalmist tells of the escape **(vv. 6–7).** He concludes with a great statement of faith, a witness and testimony to any nation that will hear: "Our help is in the name of the Lord, the Maker of heaven and earth" **(v. 8).** This is a message also for us to say today!

2. The threat to Israel is described in three word pictures: (1) Enemy nations **(vv. 2–3)** approaching the nation to swallow them all alive. Assyria and Babylon swallowed up many nations. (2) A raging torrent **(vv. 4–5)**

racing on to wash them to destruction. This latter picture is frequently used in the Bible. (See **Ps. 42:7; Ps. 69:1–2, 15; Is. 43:2.**) (3) A hunter (**vv. 6–7**)—both a predatory animal and a human using snares that almost catch a fleeing bird. The picture of being hunted as a wild animal can be seen elsewhere in the Bible. (See **Job 10:16; Prov. 6:5.**)

3. **Psalm 121** also emphasizes that true help—both for person and for nation—can only come from one source: "The Lord, the Maker of heaven and earth." In traditional liturgies, the call to worship is spoken each Sunday morning in the closing words of this psalm. After the invitation to confess their sins to God, spoken by the pastor, the congregation engages in a dialog with him. He assures us, "Our help is in the name of the Lord," and we respond, "Who made heaven and earth." The next time you participate in a worship service where this responsory is used, think of this psalm when you make your response.

B. Psalm 67—An Expression of Thanksgiving

This is a psalm encouraging peoples and nations to praise God.

1. The last two verses are the key to the reason for all the praise to be given God. Note that as God blesses, the earth produces. God gives soil, seed, sunshine, and rain. With His blessing this yields a harvest. Realizing our dependence on God, we are to fear Him and praise Him. Remember how Luther in the Catechism says, "We should fear and love God."

2. The word *may* used in most of the verses is an imperative. If you, as a leader, say to your group, "May we faithfully study before we come to our meetings," you are recommending it and challenging them to do so. This is the purpose of the psalmist also. Note all the things the psalmist encourages us to do by his appeal.

3. The psalm contains a note of missionary concern that all people to the ends of the earth may be reverent worshipers of Israel's God. God's goodness to us in and through His Son, Jesus Christ, also gives us Christians a missionary concern.

4. The first verse reminds us of the words with which Aaron was to bless the people. (Read **Num. 6:22–27.**) To "make His face [or countenance] shine upon you" is a Hebrew way of speaking of God's favor. Just as an earthly father's face beams when his child comes to him, so God's face indicates favor upon us. (See **Ps. 4:6; 44:3; 80:3.**)

Conclusion

At the close of this session try to get specific about what you can do in your own community, state or province, and nation. Ask the members to participate in prayer, thanking God for deliverance from national disaster and for guidance and protection for your nation and its leaders. Remember those young people who protect your country in its armed forces. You might even mention by name those from your own congregation. It would be a fitting close to the meeting to write, or assign individuals the responsibility of writing, to the people in service from your congregation, assuring them of your prayers for them and your country's involvement in world affairs.

Lesson 8

God Speaks about Deliverance from Trouble (Psalm 107)

Aims

To be assured that God delivers from trouble.

To thank God when we experience such deliverance and to tell others about it.

Leader's Personal Preparation

1. Do the lesson in the Study Guide before class time. Read the introduction and Bible study helps in this guide.

2. Think back to some crisis in your life and to the deliverance that came to you. Thank God again for His help, and for every day of help and blessing.

3. Think of those in your group who are facing trouble today. Breathe a prayer that this lesson may be of great help to them.

4. Study the psalm carefully and summarize what it says to you.

Introduction to the Lesson

Begin with devotions. You might read a psalm such as **Psalm 93,** which declares the everlasting power of God, as a basis for discussing the troubles of the Christian life. Pray for an understanding of God's power as you discuss this lesson.

Studying the Psalm

Read **Psalm 107.** For variety you might divide the group into four sections and read the psalm as follows:

Verses 1-3: "Give thanks"—read by all
Verses 4-9: Deliverance of lost travelers—read by group 1
Verses 10-16: Deliverance from imprisonment—read by group 2
Verses 17-22: Deliverance from sickness—read by group 3
Verses 23-32: Deliverance from storms—read by group 4
Verses 33-43: Meditation on God's providence—read by all

Let the four groups discuss the situation of distress pictured in the verses they read and find parallels in today's life, as suggested in the Study Guide. Allow plenty of time for discussion, and then have each small group share a summary with the entire group.

Discuss the other questions in each section. It is hoped that members of the group will feel free to share deliverance from crisis situations in their lives. This ought to bring you to a spirit of praise and thanksgiving by the close of the meeting.

A. Give Thanks (vv. 1-3)

As "redeemed of the Lord," we want to give thanks to our Redeemer always and in every situation. We especially praise our Savior for rescuing us from eternal death. We know that He will always deliver us.

B. Deliverance of Lost Travelers (vv. 4-9)

This could be a picture of Israel in the wilderness, hungry and thirsty, longing for a place of security and rest. When the people neglected God or rebelled against Him, they could not find their way. When they cried to the Lord, He led them until they finally reached Canaan.

We, too, are wandering through life to our eternal city. We, too, may experience that sometimes our soul faints in us and we become discouraged, frustrated, sad. When we cry to the Lord and are willing to be led by Him, He will hear us and lead us to a richer and more fruitful life.

C. Deliverance from Imprisonment (vv. 10-16)

The second group is people in captivity, prisoners, doomed to hard labor. This could be a picture of the Israelites as slaves in Egypt or of the people of Israel who were forced into captivity (by Babylon) for having rebelled against God and not having listened to His counsel. A description of this despondent condition appears in **Psalm 137.** But the people cried to the Lord, and in **Psalm 126** we read of their great joy when their bonds were broken by the Lord and they could return home.

There are forms of captivity today where people are held in prisons of unhappiness. We may be in the darkness and gloom of a destructive emotion such as fear, worry, resentment, jealousy, or hatred. Or we may be bowed down with guilt. We cannot help ourselves. We cannot by ourselves break the power of these emotions. Perhaps we do not want to cry to the Lord because we are rebelling against Him and His Word. God's Word tells us to love one another, to forgive, to pray for one another, to do good, to trust and not worry, to have time for silence, to listen to the Lord. When we spurn this counsel, we reap a breakdown of faith, of health, and of social relations. When we are willing to cry to the Lord for forgiveness, for a change of heart and mind, He brings us out of darkness. He shatters the bonds and sets us free to be happy again.

D. Deliverance from Sickness (vv. 17–22)

The third group is people who are physically sick. They are so sick that they cannot eat and are close to death. They may be reaping the harvest of sin. We can be ill for many reasons—some as a result of our own foolishness, such as wrong eating or overeating, or overactivity with not enough time to be still before the Lord. We may suffer from tension caused by emotional disorders. Our hospital beds are full of people who are "sick of it all," so sick that they need to be hospitalized. There are people who are physically ill because they have broken God's laws. Read **James 5:14–16** to see how the Lord ties together confessing of sin and being forgiven with healing.

All healing is from God. He has given us many resources to renew and sustain our daily life and to heal us when sick. He has given us fresh air and sunshine, also food and medications. He has permitted people to learn the healing arts of surgery, nursing, and therapy. Let us thank Him for all of these. **Verse 20** tells us that "He sent forth His word and healed them." His Word is full of instructions for healthful, happy living. Listen to **Prov.17:22**—"A cheerful heart is good medicine, but a crushed spirit dries up the bones." "Whoever would love life and see good days must keep his tongue from evil and his lips from deceitful speech. He must turn from evil and do good; he must seek peace and pursue it" **(1 Peter 3:10–11)**.

E. Deliverance from Storms (vv. 23–32)

The fourth group is people experiencing the dangers of sea travel—seafarers caught in a storm, about to be shipwrecked. Their courage is melting away. They are "at wits' end." But when they cried to the Lord, He stilled the storm and brought them to their desired haven.

This can apply to us in a literal way as we encounter dangers on the highways, in the air, and on the water. Before we leave on a trip, we ought always to ask the Lord to keep His everlasting arms about us and to keep us safe in His care. How comforting are the words of the hymn "Jesus, Savior, Pilot Me". Read the whole hymn for your meditation.

But whether the storms be on the sea or in our hearts, let us cry to the

Lord. He will still our storm and give us peace that "transcends all under-standing" **(Phil. 4:7)**. Then let us tell everyone who will listen how good it is to put our trust in the Lord.

F. Meditation on God's Providence (vv. 33–43)

The last part of the psalm is like a hymn of praise to God, the Lord of creation, as He deals with the wicked and the upright. He can smite the fertile land with a drought. He can transform a desert into a fertile place, thereby helping the needy and oppressed. To the wicked He can bring warning through acts in nature. To the upright He can bring a blessing. Give heed to this psalm. When you have experienced God's goodness, share what it means to have confidence in your heavenly helper.

Conclusion

Note and remember the double refrain repeated four times: "Then they cried out to the Lord in their trouble, and He delivered them from their distress" **(v. 6;** also see **vv. 13, 19,** and **28)**. "Let them give thanks to the Lord for His unfailing love and His wonderful deeds for men" **(vv. 8, 15, 21,** and **31)**. In short, the psalm is a summons to acknowledge the grace of God that we have received and to thank Him.

In keeping with the theme of giving thanks, you might close by reading **Psalm 136** antiphonally. Assign a reader to lead, and have the group respond with the phrase "His love endures forever," which concludes every verse.

Lesson 9

God Speaks about Hatred of Evildoers (Psalms 137 and 139)

Aims

To understand why the psalmists felt free to ask God to act against wicked persons who defied Him.

To see the difference between personal resentment and the hatred of forces that oppose God.

To see that Christians can love and forgive even their enemies because of Jesus.

Leader's Personal Preparation

1. Do the lesson in the Study Guide before class time. Read the introduction and Bible study helps for this lesson in this guide.

2. This lesson requires careful preparation. It discusses a difficult subject. However, it can be very profitable to you and your group. If you need further help, ask your pastor to go over this topic with you. Remember, however, that you are not expected to have all the answers. You are the leader to guide discussion and occasionally weave in what others may not have known or seen.

3. Pray for understanding. Pray for a profitable group study. This is an important study because quite a number of psalms have imprecatory sections. (To *imprecate* means "to pray for evil or misfortune upon an enemy.")

4. Make a list for yourself of evil forces in your community or in your country that work destruction of life or character. Also make a list of groups that are doing something to stem the tide of evil.

Introduction to the Lesson

Begin with devotions. You might use the portion from the Sermon on the Mount that deals with love for enemies **(Matt. 5:43–48).**

Explain the purpose of imprecatory psalms. This could be accomplished by having someone read the introductory paragraph in the "Purpose" section of the Study Guide. You might draw attention particularly to **Psalm 139,** where the imprecatory section is only a small portion of the entire psalm. Hatred toward evildoers should be looked at only in terms of the whole of Christian life.

The imprecatory sections of the psalms will take on meaning as you and your group seek to distinguish between resentment of people and hatred of forces that destroy humankind, always remembering that the psalms do not use New Testament language.

Studying the Psalms

A. Psalm 137: A Psalm of Love and Hate

This psalm is a lament of an individual for his people, who were in the Babylonian captivity. He thinks back not only to his own experiences in exile but also to those of the whole group of exiles. Thus he writes, "*We* sat and wept" **(v. 1).**

In reading **Psalm 137** you could divide the participants into two sections, the first group reading **verses 1–6** regarding love, and the second group reading **verses 7–9** regarding hate. You might have each group discuss their section and share some of their thinking with the entire class.

Following this, discuss the questions posed in the Study Guide.

1. The people of Israel had been taken captive by the Babylonians. Their place of exile (vv. 1–2) is designated only as "by the rivers of Babylon." These were the Tigris and the Euphrates rivers with their network of canals, on whose banks grew a special kind of poplar trees. On them the exiles hung their harps because they were too sad to play them.

2. Note the picture of dejection. (a) The people sat down and wept; (b) They remembered Zion (Jerusalem with its temple service); (c) Their tormentors, mocking their songs, which they once sang in the temple, coaxed them to sing the psalms for entertainment in spite of their weeping.

3. To be forced to live in a foreign land was bad enough, but to forget the homeland would have been treason. The psalmist loved Jerusalem with its temple and the altar of God so deeply that he wanted to do something patriotic. He had to resist the enemies of Zion. The only way he knew they could be overthrown was that God would curse them.

4. The psalmist prayed, "Remember, O Lord, what the Edomites did on the day Jerusalem fell. 'Tear it down,' they cried" (v. 7). He wished a curse on Babylon (vv. 8–9). This curse takes the form of a blessing upon any nation that will pay back to Babylon according to the law of retaliation. This Old Testament law, found in Ex. 21:24; Lev. 24:20; and Deut. 19:21, says that an eye should be given for an eye, a tooth for a tooth, a hand for a hand, a foot for a foot, a wound for a wound, and a life for a life. If we had lived under the Old Testament teaching, we too would probably have felt as the psalmist did.

5. To us of the New Testament age, who know the law of love and forgiveness, such a spirit of retaliation is not appropriate. Christ had not yet come when this psalm was written. The psalmist had never heard Christ's gracious words "Love your enemies, do good to those who hate you, bless those who curse you, pray for those who mistreat you" (Luke 6:27–28). Paul had not yet written his wonderful letter to the Romans with advice as to ways of overcoming an enemy with love (Rom. 12:9–21).

6–7. Discuss what actions Christians can take today against the enemies of God.

B. Psalm 139: A Wise Man's Prayer

This psalm is one of the great psalms, sections of which are well known. It is a magnificent tribute to the greatness of God. The psalmist is saying, in effect, "My God, how great Thou art."

You may wish to divide the group again for the reading of Psalm 139. Since we are concerned in this study with imprecatory psalms, first have the entire group read the section in verses 19–24. Talk briefly about the last two verses in relation to this section, where it seems that the psalmist is asking God to assure him of the rightness of his hatred. Following this, read the entire psalm, a section at a time, and talk briefly about each section. Then discuss the questions relative to this psalm. Encourage members of the group to share enrichment that may have come to them from their study at home and challenge them to do more and more of this type of study.

1. "You know me." God's omniscience (**vv. 1–6**).
David sees himself as one whom God has examined and knows thoroughly. God knows him when he is at rest or at work. God even knows what he is going to say before he has said it. God's presence surrounds David at all times. Such infinite knowledge is beyond human understanding.

2. "You are there." God's omnipresence (**vv. 7–12**).
Earlier in his life David might have felt like fleeing from God on account of his deep sense of sin. But in these verses he is glorying in God's nearness. There is no place where one can hide from God: heaven, the depths (Sheol—region of the dead), wings of the dawn (that is, to follow the first rays of the morning sun, which stretch like outspread wings to the far horizon), darkness. Read **Jer. 23:23–24** for another beautiful passage about God's omnipresence.

3. "You created." God's omnipotence (**vv. 13–18**).
The psalmist praises God, not by enumerating all His mighty acts in creation and history, but by telling of the marvel of God's creation of him as a person. When he awakens, he finds that he is still with God.

4. Prayer for God to slay the wicked (**vv. 19–22**).
The wicked in this instance were men of war who also defied God. The psalmist lived so close to God that the thought of those who defied Him and shed blood was unbearable. Encourage the participants to express why the attitude of Christians toward enemies is different.

5. Prayer against God's enemies (**vv. 21–22**).
The psalmist saw the wicked as God's enemies and therefore his own enemies, who should be destroyed. Jesus inspires us to love our enemies and pray for them.

6. Prayer for himself (**vv. 23–24**).
Aware of his own imperfection, the psalmist asks God to examine him further—even though, according to **verse 2,** God knows all about him. Then he asks God to guide him through life.

C. Deliverance from Evildoers, Then and Now
1. When in the Lord's Prayer we pray, "Thy kingdom come, Thy will be

done," and "deliver us from evil," we are also asking God to deal with evildoers.

"Thy kingdom come," we pray, and we remember that the kingdom has enemies who seek to hinder the spread of the Gospel. In actual practice, evil and evildoers are inseparable. So when we pray and God answers our prayer, judgment must strike those who do the evil.

"Thy will be done on earth," we pray, and we line ourselves up on God's side, asking Him to destroy and bring to naught every evil counsel and purpose of the devil, the world, and our own flesh that would hinder the coming of His kingdom. Many careless and evil people resist the will of God. When we ask God to hinder or change them, we also are resisting evil, with the well-being of God's kingdom in mind. This is not in a spirit of personal revenge.

"Deliver us from evil," we pray. It is evil people who do evil actions. When we ask to be delivered from them, we are praying for their overthrow. In our day we think of the evil experienced by modern martyrs in the form of torture, brainwashing, concentration camps, and death at the hands of evil people. When we ask God to deliver us from evil, we ask to be delivered from evil people. So we, too, ask God to resist, to overthrow, to bring to judgment all who are His enemies.

2. The New Testament way is different in that it includes forgiveness and hope for the salvation of the evildoers. We don't ask for death, but newness of life. This should be our continual prayer.

Conclusion

In closing, read **Rom. 12:9** and pray for wisdom to know what is evil in God's sight and how to hate it righteously. Ask for guidance to know where we can be used to correct evil situations.

Lesson 10

God Speaks about Doubt
(Psalm 73)

Aim

To learn how to overcome doubt.

Leader's Personal Preparation

1. This psalm is not an easy one because it deals with the problem of

doubt, which is a difficult topic. Therefore, do careful and prayerful preparation.

2. Read the instructions for the leader at the beginning of this guide.

3. Do the lesson in the Study Guide before class time. Read the introduction and Bible study helps in this guide.

4. Try to think of times in your life when you were puzzled by doubts and crises that you had to face. Perhaps you, too, wondered if God knew and cared, and why He didn't act. This will make the psalmist's words seem as if they have been written for you.

5. Carefully schedule what you are going to do according to the time available.

Introduction to the Lesson

Begin with devotions. A good passage to set the mood of the study is **Ps. 37:1–11.**

Have the group read the psalm together. Proceed through the items for discussion, giving plenty of time to relate them to present-day life and any problems anyone may have. Stress the problem of doubt, which is prevalent among all people regardless of age or background. It is hoped that from the study of this psalm a clear understanding of how to overcome doubt will be seen. It might be important to emphasize the danger of sharing doubts with everyone unless you have come back to faith and have seen the results of such questioning and uncertainty.

Studying the Psalm

When we spend too much time trying to understand God's ways, we get weary and confused. With God in our hearts we don't need answers to our "whys." He is our answer. Read **Is. 55:6–9** and note that we are not able to fathom God's thoughts and ways, but yet we dare to trust Him. Now read **Jer. 29:11–13.** It would be well for you to memorize these two wonderful passages.

A. God Is Good (vv. 1–3)

The psalmist mentions those to whom God is good: (1) "Israel." We would probably say "the believers." Note how honest the psalmist is. He tells us how he almost lost faith in God. Total honesty before God is a necessity for prayer. Being honest with ourselves releases us from the need to make excuses or to deny our weaknesses. (2) "Those who are pure in heart." During worship we pray, "Create in me a clean heart." We know our hearts are not clean, but they can be cleansed through Christ's forgiveness. Note God's promise in **Matt. 5:8** to the pure in heart.

All people of God have weak moments and blind spots. Asaph's was his jealous envy of the prosperous wicked.

B. The Prosperity of the Wicked (vv. 4–9)

In the dark night of doubt, the psalmist lost his sense of true values. The temporary, present life with earthly glitter blinded him to inner, spiritual joy. He was tempted to give up his faith and join the ranks of the wicked, who were wealthy and at ease. He thought they never had troubles (v. 5), yet they were guilty of pride, violence, scoffing, malice, arrogance, and oppression (vv. 6–9).

C. People Are Led Astray by the Example of the Wicked (vv. 10–12)

Many people are led astray by the example of the wicked and become atheists themselves (vv. 10–11). Their question "How can God know?" has found its dreary echo in human hearts in all generations. According to the psalmist, godless persons appear to be carefree and always gaining in wealth.

D. The Psalmist Is Frustrated (vv. 13–16)

The psalmist feels that his godly life has been in vain, since he has faced continual chastening (vv. 13–14). The more he dwells on this, the more oppressed he feels.

Fortunately the psalmist did not parade his doubt in the presence of others. If he had, he would have been a traitor to God's children. He pictured to himself a generation growing up bereft of ideals, without spiritual consciousness, living for material ends alone. At this thought he was seized with sickening horror. What a hell this world would be if it were populated by a race totally destitute of faith in God. Something within his soul checked him from saying how he felt. But he still struggled with the question of God's fairness. Vice didn't seem to bring any penalty of pain, but rather much profit. The wicked were happy in life and untroubled in their death. Yet he, being honest with God and seeking to live the godly life, had troubles.

E. Turning Point (v. 17)

The word *till* brings the psalmist out of the dark night of doubt into the bright day of faith. He did what God in **Ps. 46:10** suggests when there is commotion around us: "Be still, and know that I am God." The psalmist did just that. He went into the sanctuary and was still before God. Other things grew strangely dim in the light of His glory and grace.

The *sanctuary* experience has several possible explanations: (1) It might have happened as he was alone in the temple, quiet, at leisure, conversing with God, that a flash of light or insight from God came to him. In the stillness God had a chance to show Asaph what he couldn't grasp while he was griping. (2) This experience might have come when he was in the temple for a public service with other worshipers. Through the liturgy, prayers, lessons, etc., his mind was lifted to final issues. He had been in the tyranny of trifles. Now he saw all from a spiritual point of view. He saw that what he had envied was cheap delusion. (3) He might have been in the sanctuary of God's Word, alone with God's message. God was his teacher through the Scriptures. A passage of Scripture can be the place to get a new lease on life, a new sense of values, a new dedication to God.

F. The End of the Wicked (vv. 18–20)

What Asaph saw was that the wicked and their prosperity do not last and that they live in a dream world of false security, unconcerned about the end of life. **Verse 18** is a picture of the wicked separated from God. Their contentment is temporary. They rush to a blind and terrible end.

G. The Difference in Asaph (vv. 21–26)

Asaph now sees that his former bitterness was an evidence of his sinful stupidity and beastliness.

The most important truth for Asaph (and for us) is this: *We are not alone.* What we need is not an *explanation* but a God who is involved in these things with us. He has not deserted us. We are not dependent solely on our own poor resources—and how very poor they are! All mysteries are not solved by the cross, but its power to overcome becomes our power. In **verse 23** Asaph says that God holds him by his right hand. The picture of God holding our hand is often used in Scriptures. For comfort and joy read these passages: **Is. 41:10, 13; John 10:27–28.** What is promised to those who are with God now? (Note **Ps. 32:8; 23:4.**) Afterward? (Note **John 14:2–3.**)

H. A Contrast (vv. 27–28)

In **verse 28** Asaph declares that it is good to be with or near God. In a number of passages we are invited to come near Him. Read the following: **James 4:8; Is. 55:1, 6;** and **Heb. 10:22.**

In **verse 28** the psalmist's last words are a desire to tell others of all God's works. He has a story to tell: the highest good in life is to be near God.

Conclusion

Psalm 1 might be read as a fitting closing. You might have one group read **verses 1–3,** which picture the happiness of the godly, and another group read **verses 4–6,** which describe the misery of the wicked. Close with prayer, thanking God for His faithfulness, asking for forgiveness through Christ for all shortcomings and doubts, and asking for renewed faith in His steadfast love.

Lesson 11

God Speaks about Thanksgiving
(Psalm 92)

Aims

To learn what can be included in a prayer of thanksgiving.
To be reminded that it is good to give thanks to God.

Leader's Personal Preparation

1. Read the instructions for the leader at the beginning of this guide.

2. Do the lesson in the Study Guide before class time. Read the introduction and Bible study helps in this guide.

3. You will want to be spiritually prepared to lead your group in Bible study, as well as to be fully informed. Ask God to give you a greater capacity to feel and express gratitude every day of your life. Ask Him to give you the wisdom and understanding you will need to lead this study. Also you will need facts. Therefore, be faithful in answering questions and in thinking through the discussion suggestions. Do good homework.

4. When you have finished this, close your books and put into one sentence what you want to remember from this psalm.

Introduction to the Lesson

Begin with devotions. You might set the tone of the meeting with some other psalms or poems of thanksgiving. The group might sing the doxology, or this might be used at the close of the meeting.

Read the psalm in its entirety and then reread it, a portion at a time, entering into the discussion questions that apply to that portion of the psalm. You might divide your group into smaller groups for this discussion before they all discuss the section.

Ask members of the group to share portions of other psalms of thanksgiving with which they are familiar. If no one has a portion to share with others, you might ask everyone to look at **Psalm 111.** Have everyone read it together and note the many things for which to be thankful. Discuss levels of maturity in giving thanks. Discuss particularly the ability to give thanks even for difficult situations in life. Try to draw out of the participants some experiences they have had in this respect.

Studying the Psalm

A. It Is Good to Praise the Lord (vv. 1–4)

1. In Bible study every word is important to us. We get the deeper meaning as we look at words and sentence structure. Note in **verses 1–2** that in praising the Lord the psalmist gave thanks and proclaimed God's love and faithfulness. We may express our praise and gratitude to God through music or through telling others of God's goodness. Another necessity in Bible study is to know the meaning of words. Therefore, although we think we know what it means to "proclaim," we look it up in the dictionary and find that it means to "announce openly or say emphatically." This is what the psalmist did, and we must too.

2. By referring to God as "O Most High," the psalmist asserts that there is only one God, who is over everything.

3. The psalmist stresses the morning and evening time for proclaiming God's love, probably because that's when the daily burnt offerings were made. (See **Ex. 29:38–42** and **Num. 28:1–8**.) The musical instruments mentioned in **verse 3** were used in the temple service.

The word *for* (**v. 4**) could be interpreted *because*. The psalmist is grateful for God's work. He seems to express thanks for some specific "deeds" on his behalf, something God did for or to him, and also generally for the works of His hands in creation.

B. The Greatness of God's Works (vv. 5–11)

1. In **verse 5** the psalmist repeats the greatness of God's works. This verse reminds us of the honor given God in **Psalm 19** as the Creator having completed His handiwork.

But God is not only great in creation; His thoughts are beyond our understanding. As Paul wrote to the Romans, we can only exclaim, "Oh, the depth of the riches of the wisdom and knowledge of God! How unsearchable His judgments, and His paths beyond tracing out! . . . For from Him and through Him and to Him are all things. To Him be the glory forever! Amen" (**Rom. 11:33, 36**).

2. The Hebrew word translated *fools* denotes those who are morally—not mentally—deficient. These people are too wrapped up in their sin to see that God has offered them a way out.

3. Note the contrast between the fate of the evildoers ("forever destroyed") and the Lord, who will be "exalted forever."

4. **Verse 10** has symbolic language (representing a truth by means of an object; e.g., the dove is a symbol of peace, a flag is a symbol of a country) to show how God has dealt with the psalmist. He made him strong like the wild ox. The *horn* is a symbol of strength. The psalmist explains that the Lord's salvation is like being anointed with fresh oil. This may refer to festive anointing with perfumed oil (see **Ps. 23:5** and **Ps. 45:7**), to the priest's anointing of a sick man (see **Lev. 14:10–20**), or to God's strength and blessing, which is poured out upon His children.

5. The salvation of the Lord includes total victory over one's enemies—especially over sin, death, and the devil.

C. Prosperity of the Righteous (vv. 12–15)

Varying figures are used to describe prosperity: (a) the palm tree, upright, able to flourish amid drought of the desert, ever green, useful in its fruit-bearing; (b) the cedar of Lebanon, tall, beautiful, long-lived. One further fact of interest about the palm tree is that, instead of adding a new outer ring to the trunk every year, it grows inwardly from the center. So indeed it is with the true Christian. Vital Christianity is an inward renewal by the Holy Spirit, an inward sanctification of heart, and an inward development of character, which then outwardly manifests itself in uprightness, beauty, and fruitfulness. Like the palm tree or the cedar, the righteous flourish in the presence of the Lord. Even in old age they are fruitful and very much alive.

Conclusion

In closing you may wish to have the group read **Psalm 117,** which is a great burst of praise for God's steadfast love.

Lesson 12

God Speaks When I Think of the Passing of Time (Psalm 90)

Aims

To see the brevity of our existence.
To appreciate God's timelessness.
To become wise stewards of time.

Leader's Personal Preparation

1. As you get ready for your study, review quickly how God has protected you, provided for you, and led you. Think of the people in your study group. Ask God to speak to you and to them through this psalm.
2. Read the instructions for the leader at the beginning of this guide.
3. Do the lesson in the Study Guide before class time. Read the introduction and Bible study helps in this guide.
4. Read the aims for this study. Keep them in mind. They will help to open up the message of the psalm.
5. Look up the meaning of any word you do not understand.

Introduction to the Lesson

Begin with devotions. Have the group read the psalm.

Adapt this lesson to the unique situation in your group. If time permits, take each section of the psalm and discuss the related items as you proceed through the psalm. If time is brief, you may wish to assign the different sections to small groups for discussion. At the end they may briefly share their thinking with the others.

Studying the Psalm

"Our God, our help in ages past, Our hope for years to come,
Our shelter from the stormy blast, And our eternal home:
Before the hills in order stood Or earth received its frame,
From everlasting You are God, To endless years the same"

With these words the hymn writer Isaac Watts (1674–1748) summed up for the people of his generation the message of **Psalm 90.**

The setting of this psalm might have been a congregation at prayer on a fast day or the period after some national calamity.

A. Human Life Is Short; God Is Eternal (vv. 1–6)

Moses looked back in awe and wonder at how God dealt with individuals and peoples. Mountains are specifically named because they are regarded as the oldest parts of the earth. (See **Deut. 33:15; Hab. 3:6.**)

In **verses 5–6** we see God removing many persons, and we think of the loss of life in a natural disaster. Then we see people wither as individual blades of grass, each when his or her evening has come. Scriptures frequently use the picture of fields of grass or flowers. (See **Is. 40:6–8; Ps. 103:15–16; 1 Peter 1:24; Luke 12:28; James 1:10.**)

B. God's Displeasure with Sin (vv. 7–12)

To understand these verses better, it will help to be reminded of Paul's statement in **Rom. 5:12:** "Therefore, just as sin entered the world through one man, and death through sin, . . . in this way death came to all men, because all sinned." (See also **Rom. 6:23.**)

Although we read in **Deut. 34:7** that Moses lived 120 years, in this psalm he mentions 70 to 80 years as the normal life expectancy. But as we read the whole psalm, we sense that the purpose of his poem is not so much to make a study of the length of life as to remind us to be grateful for the security we have in God's care during our short life.

Verse 11 is difficult. It can be paraphrased: "Who understands Your anger against sin so as to give You fitting and holy reverence?" Moses would remind us that, although God is our dwelling place, when we reject Him and choose a life of unconfessed sin, this sin must be dealt with. God resists evil with great power and wrath. Therefore, let us fear and love God, aware of our responsibility for our conduct and character. God's displeasure with us is in proportion to our failure to yield to Him our obedience and the reverence that is His right.

C. A Prayer for God's Forgiveness and Favor (vv. 13–17)

The psalmist prays for God's favor. (See **Ps. 5:12; Ps. 30:5; Prov. 8:35.**)

"Establish the work of our hands" means praying for blessing on our daily life and occupation. To establish is to make firm, stable, and permanent.

Moses ends his psalm with a prayer for God's mercy and blessing. He ends as he began on the triumphant note of trust in God, who was his dwelling place. Calendars and clocks cannot ultimately hold us in bondage. Our God is eternal, and we shall spend eternity with Him, thanks to Jesus' cross and empty tomb. In light of this, every day of our life should count for eternity. We ought to evaluate all we do in the light of life's shortness and eternity's endlessness.

Conclusion

In closing you may wish to have the members write an appropriate prayer that could be read, or you may ask someone to close with prayer.

Find Heali~~~   *Chris*~~~ **an Support Studies**
for Individuals
or Groups

THE
MA~~~
To~~~

*J*esus' hea~~~
    and forgi~~~
    positive ~~~
weighing on ~~~
and share H~~~
will lead yo~~~
maturity an~~~
ences, and e~~~
who face simi~~~

Living ~~~   *viors*
Suffe~~~   *rce*
Livin~~~
Coping with~~~

© CPH 1994   H54920/2